Push your Career Publish your Thesis

Science should be accessible to everybody. Share the knowledge, the ideas, and the passion about your research. Give your part of the infinite amount of scientific research possibilities a finite frame.

Publish your examination paper, diploma thesis, bachelor thesis, master thesis, dissertation, or habilitation treatises in form of a book.

A finite frame by infinite science.

An Imprint of
Infinite Science GmbH
MFC 1 | Technikzentrum Lübeck
BioMedTec Wissenschaftscampus
Maria-Goeppert-Straße 1
23562 Lübeck
book@infinite-science.de
www.infinite-science.de

Editor

Thorsten M. Buzug
Institute of Medical Engineering
University of Lübeck
buzug@imt.uni-luebeck.de

Reihe: Medizinische Ingenieurwissenschaft und Biomedizintechnik

Diese Reihe umfasst Werke der Medizinischen In-
genieurwissenschaft und Biomedizintechnik, deren
Themen strategisch unter den Zukunftstechnologien
mit hohem Innovationspotenzial anzusiedeln sind. Als
wesentliche Trends dieser Forschungsgebiete, sind die
Schlüsselbereiche Computerisierung, Miniaturisierung
und Molekularisierung zu nennen. Bei der Computerisierung sind dabei die inhaltlichen Schwerpunkte
beispielsweise in der Bildgebung und Bildverarbeitung
gegeben. Die Miniaturisierung spielt unter anderem
bei intelligenten Implantaten, der minimalinvasiven
Chirurgie aber auch bei der Entwicklung von neuen na-
nostrukturierten Materialien eine wichtige Rolle, und
die Molekularisierung ist in der regenerativen Medizin
aber auch im Rahmen der sogenannten molekularen
Bildgebung ein entscheidender Aspekt. Forschungs-
und Entwicklungspotenzial werden auch der Biophoto-
nik und der minimal-invasiven Chirurgie unter Berück-
sichtigung der Robotik und Navigation zugeschrieben.
Querschnittstechnologien wie die Mikrosystemtech-
nik, optische Technologien, Softwaresysteme und Wis-
senstechnologien sind dabei von hohem Interesse.

Florian Griese

X-Space Reconstruction with Lissajous Trajectories in Magnetic Particle Imaging

Medical Engineering Science and
Biomedical Engineering — Volume 13

Editor: Thorsten M. Buzug

Infinite Science
Publishing

© 2015 Infinite Science Publishing
der BioMedTec Wissenschaftsverlag Lübeck

Ein Imprint der Infinite Science GmbH,
MFC 1 | BioMedTec Wissenschaftscampus
Maria-Goeppert-Straße 1
23562 Lübeck

Cover Design, Illustration: Uli Schmidts, metonym
Copy Editing: University of Lübeck, Institute of Medical Engineering

Publisher: Infinite Science GmbH, Lübeck, www.infinite-science.de
Print: BoD, Norderstedt

ISBN Paperback:978-3-945954-14-0

Bibliografische Information der Deutschen Nationalbibliothek:
Die Deutsche Nationalbibliothek verzeichnet diese Publikation in der Deutschen Nationalbibliografie; detaillierte bibliografische Daten sind im Internet über http://dnb.d-nb.de abrufbar.

Bibliographic information published by the Deutsche Nationalbibliothek
The Deutsche Nationalbibliothek lists this publication in the Deutsche Nationalbibliografie; detailed bibliographic data are available in the internet at http://dnb.d-nb.de.

ABSTRACT

Magnetic particle imaging is a recently introduced medical imaging modality. The method promises high sensitivity, high resolution and real-time ability by imaging the distribution of super-paramagnetic nanoparticles. To date, different reconstruction techniques have been presented and performed while they can be distinguished into two main categories, the frequency and the x-space reconstruction. In this work, a comparison between both techniques is made based on a simulation study. The x-space reconstruction technique using the Lissajous trajectory is presented for various parameters for an ideal scanner. Furthermore, the deconvolution process for the x-space reconstruction is performed with two deconvolving techniques, the Tikhonov and the Wiener deconvolution. Frequency reconstruction and x-space reconstruction are compared in terms of different setups regarding the density of the trajectory, gradient strength and sampling frequency for an ideal scanner and a realistic scanner with classical coil geometry. The advantages and disadvantages of both reconstruction techniques are analysed in detail.

ZUSAMMENFASSUNG

Magnetic Particle Imaging ist eine kürzlich neu vorgestellte Bildgebungsmethode. Sie verspricht eine hohe Sensitivität, eine hohe Auflösung und hat die Eigenschaft, die Verteilung von superparamagnetischen Nanopartikeln in Echtzeit darstellen zu können. Bis heute wurden verschiedene Rekonstruktionstechniken vorgestellt und umgesetzt, wobei man zwei Kategorien unterscheiden kann: die frequenzraumbasierte und die zeitraumbasierte Rekonstruktion. In dieser Arbeit wird ein Vergleich zwischen beiden Techniken unternommen basierend auf einer Simulationsstudie. Die zeitraumbasierte Rekonstruktionstechnik wird mit einer Lissajous-Trajektorie für verschiedene Parameter auf einem idealen Scanner simuliert. Des Weiteren wird der Entfaltungsprozess für die zeitraumbasierte Rekonstruktion mit zwei verschiedenen Entfaltungstechniken, der Tikhonov- und der Wiener Entfaltung, analysiert. Die frequenzraumbasierte und die zeitraumbasierte Rekonstruktion werden auf Grundlage von verschiedener Dichte der Trajektorie, unterschiedlicher Gradienten Stärke und variirender Abtastrate für einen idealen und einen realistischen Scanner verglichen. Nachfolgend werden die Vor- und Nachteile von beiden Rekonstruktionstechniken im Detail analysiert.

Contents

1 Introduction

Magnetic particle imaging (MPI) is a quantitative imaging modality and has been presented by Gleich et al. [1] in 2005. The technique is able to visualize the distribution of superparamagnetic iron oxide (SPIO) nanoparticles with the help of its nonlinear magnetic characteristics.

MPI is able of a high spatial resolution in the sub-millimeter range [2] and a high temporal resolution with 40 volumes per second [3]. The resolution of MPI is defined by the magnetic characteristic of the SPIO nanoparticles and by the strength of an applied magnetic field. By using MPI, no ionizing radiation as in positron emission tomography (PET) or iodine tracer agents are used, which are causing problems for patients with poor kidney function.

An ideal application for MPI would be blood flow quantification [3]. The technique would visualize only the tracer within the blood vessel and no surrounding tissue. In order to have an anatomical tissue structure, MPI needs to be combined with magnetic resonance imaging (MRI) or computed tomography (CT). The gold standard x-ray fluoroscopy and CT angiography rely on a catheterized arterial injection with a high concentration of iodine to achieve a high contrast. Patients with chronic kidney disease (CKD) are at risk to suffer from contrast-induced nephropathy (CIN) [4]. In MPI the iron oxide tracers are processed in the liver and not in the kidneys [5] ,[6]. Further applications for MPI could be the sentinel lymph node detection [7] and the catheter visualization [8].

The physical fundamentals rely on nonlinear magnetic characteristics of the nanoparticles when they are excited by an applied oscillating magnetic field. The nanoparticles cause a responding change of the magnetization that induces a voltage signal in the receive coils. The oscillating magnetic field is called drive field. In order to achieve spatial encoding, an additional magnetic gradient field is superposed to the drive field. It generates the field-free point (FFP). The FFP is moved by the drive field through the field of view (FOV) and ensures that the received signal comes only from the specified position of the FFP.

As a next step, the distribution of the nanoparticle concentration has to be reconstructed to an image of the FOV. It is assumed that the particle-particle interaction is negligible and then the imaging process can be described by a linear integral equation. The integral kernel formulates the relation between received signal and particle response. This connection is denoted as the system function in the analytical form and as the system matrix in the discrete form.

First promising results by [1], [9], [10] have been used the system matrix and used the measurement approach. The measurement approach means that the system matrix is obtained by a robot moving a particle sample through each position of the field of view. That makes this approach very time consuming.

Another possibility to acquire the system matrix is realized by modeling the system function. In that case the computation of the system matrix is based on the physical model. The results have been published by [11], [12], where non-ideal magnetic field shapes have been considered.

All presented techniques suffer from some drawbacks that come along with the system matrix. If the measurement approach is used, the acquisition time becomes very long. Furthermore, the system matrix needs extensive storage in the memory and the inversion of the system matrix, which is equivalent to the reconstruction time, is quite time consuming. In most publications the signal has been transformed to frequency space in order to perform the reconstruction.

A different approach of the MPI imaging equation has been presented in [13], where the MPI imaging equation is formulated as a convolution. But the formulation as convolution assumes ideal magnetic fields and an ideal magnetization response of the nanoparticles. The same approach has been published in [14], [15], [16] with an adjusted convolution kernel. The reconstruction technique is called x-space, since the reconstruction is done in time domain and the signal is not transformed with the Fourier transformation.

In this work, the x-space reconstruction is performed with four different phantoms for various parameters such as density of the trajectory, gradient and sampling rate. The deconvolution process of the x-space reconstruction is studied extensively, while two different approaches are compared namely the deconvolution with Tikhonov regularization and the Wiener deconvolution. The frequency reconstruction and the x-space reconstruction are compared based on a simulation study. The different methods are analysed in detail and their advantages and disadvantages are demonstrated. Their reconstruction results are compared in terms of different parameter combinations and for different coil setups such as the ideal scanner and the classical coil setup.

2 Fundamentals

In this chapter the physical fundamentals in MPI are presented in order to understand the aspects analysed in this work.

At first, the Maxwell equations for static magnetic fields and slowly changing magnetic fields are explained in section 2.1. The skin effect and the induction in thick wires are formulated to underline the necessity for litz wire in the coils. Then, the signal encoding process in MPI is presented in section 2.2 and it is shown with the help of the Langevin function. The spatial encoding is achieved with a static selection field and furthermore the field-free point is explained in section 2.3. The characteristics of the magnetic nanoparticles are presented in section 2.4 and their importance for the MPI imaging process. The Lissajous trajectory is analysed in detail with its advantages and disadvantages in section 2.5. The phase shift method is shown to compensate the disadvantage of a fixed excitation frequency and the difference between sinusoidal and triangular excitation is discussed. The prospects of resolution and sensitivity in MPI are described and the connection between gradient, particle size and trajectory is studied in section 2.6. The signal chain for MPI is given in a summarized form in section 2.7.

2.1 Magnetization

The four Maxwell equations for classical electrodynamics describe the fundamental relation between moving charges and time varying electric and magnetic fields. Electrostatics is a special case of electrodynamics and deals with nonmoving electric charges and constant static electric fields. The assumption of electrostatics can also be applied for moving electric charges as long as the velocity and acceleration of the charges are small and the variation of the electric field is negligible.

Magnetostatics is also a special case of the electrodynamics and describes constant currents and their resulting magnetic fields. The terms and laws of magnetostatics can also be used when the current changes slowly in the conductor and the magnetic field changes less magnificently.

In MPI the theory of magnetostatics is sufficient and can be used to explain its functionality.

The electric field plays only a minor roll and the currents in the conductor, which generate the magnetic field, are nearly constant. For the changing magnetic field in MPI the induction term of the Maxwell equation is relevant to explain the skin effect and the induction.

The quasistatic approximation is applied since the velocity of the current is small compared to the speed of light. A more detailed explanation and discussion of more conditions can be found in [17].

2.1.1 Magnetostatics

The basic equations of magnetostatics for magnetic fields in vacuum are described by the Maxwell equations

$$\text{div } \boldsymbol{B} = \nabla \boldsymbol{B} = 0, \quad \text{rot } \frac{\boldsymbol{B}}{\mu_0} = \nabla \times \frac{\boldsymbol{B}}{\mu_0} = \boldsymbol{j} + \frac{\partial \epsilon_0 \boldsymbol{E}}{\partial t}, \tag{2.1.1}$$

where $\boldsymbol{B}$ is the magnetic flux density and $\boldsymbol{j}$ the current density. The magnetic field constant is given by μ_0 and the electric field constant is denoted with ϵ_0 with its electric field $\boldsymbol{E}$. With the condition of dissolving time derivatives $\frac{\partial}{\partial t} \equiv 0$ the simplified Maxwell equations are then given by

$$\text{div } \boldsymbol{B} = \nabla \cdot \boldsymbol{B} = 0, \quad \text{rot } \frac{\boldsymbol{B}}{\mu_0} = \nabla \times \frac{\boldsymbol{B}}{\mu_0} = \boldsymbol{j}. \tag{2.1.2}$$

The first equation also known as Gauss's law means that the vector field is source-free and that its magnetic field lines do not have a starting point. It also underlines the fact that there are no magnetic monopoles [18], [19]. The second equation also known as Ampère's law states that a current density $\boldsymbol{j}$ in a conductor induces a proportional right turning magnetic field around the conductor.

The magnetic flux density $\boldsymbol{B}$ can generally be written as a rotation of a vector potential with a vector function $\boldsymbol{A}$

$$\boldsymbol{B} = \text{rot } \boldsymbol{A} = \nabla \times \boldsymbol{A} \tag{2.1.3}$$

when the current distribution $\boldsymbol{j}(\boldsymbol{l})$ is unknown [18]. The magnetic induction $\boldsymbol{B}$ can be estimated by the Biot-Savart law

$$\boldsymbol{B}(\boldsymbol{r}) = \frac{\mu_0}{4\pi} \int_V \frac{\boldsymbol{j}(\boldsymbol{l}) \times (\boldsymbol{r} - \boldsymbol{l})}{||\boldsymbol{r} - \boldsymbol{l}||_2^3} d^3l \tag{2.1.4}$$

when the current density $\boldsymbol{j}(\boldsymbol{l})$ is known and $\boldsymbol{r}$ describes the local position with the relative position $\boldsymbol{l}$.

The Biot-Savart law is discretized and implemented in the later explained simulation tool and more information about the Biot-Savart-law can be found in [18], [19], [17].

2.1.2 Skin effect and induction

The skin effect appears in time depending current distributions and has to be avoided since the current will flow mainly at the surface and will increase the resistance in the conductor. The current in the conductor will generate a changing magnetic field within the conductor. In turn, the changing magnetic field will induce an eddy current which runs in the opposite direction of the main current direction.

The current is forced to flow at the surface since the magnetic field becomes the strongest in the center of the conductor. The skin effect is depending on the frequency of the alternating current and of the cross-section of the conductor. For further information regarding the skin depth and current density in a conductor, the literature [17], [18], [19] is revealing.

In magnetic particle imaging the skin effect would cause heat problems since the resistance would be increased and therefore the heat development would be much stronger. A cooling systems would probably become necessary. The problem is solved by coils which are winded with very thin litz wire. The litz wire minimise the skin effect. The skin effect is also avoided by litz wire in the receive coils. There the skin effect would cause unwanted noise.

The induction as mentioned before is caused by a time changing magnetic flux density $\boldsymbol{B}(\boldsymbol{r}, t)$. It can be derived [18] that the voltage $u(t)$ in a close circuit is described by the first time deviation of the magnetic flux ϕ_O over the surface O and is connected to $\boldsymbol{B}(\boldsymbol{r}, t)$ by

$$u(t) = -\frac{\partial \phi_O}{\partial t} = -\frac{\partial}{\partial t} \int_O \boldsymbol{B}(\boldsymbol{r}, t) \cdot d\boldsymbol{A}. \tag{2.1.5}$$

The voltage $u(t)$ is therefore proportional to the deviated magnetic flux.

This connection explains the generated response of the magnetic particle as voltage in the receive coils.

2.2 Signal encoding in MPI

The SPIO nanoparticles are excited by a sinusoidal oscillating magnetic field

$$\boldsymbol{H}_{AC}(t) = H_0 sin(2\pi f_0 t) \tag{2.2.1}$$

where H_0 is the amplitude, f_0 is the frequency and $\boldsymbol{H}_{AC}(t)$ meaning that the magnetic field is generated by an alternating current (AC). This alternating field is called drive field. A schematical depiction as the sinusoidal oscillation can be seen in figure 2.1 (left). The drive field can

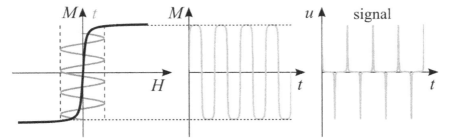

Figure 2.1: Signal encoding: The alternating drive field (red) changes the magnetization of the nanoparticles continuously (left) and the nanoparticles respond with an alternating magnetization $\boldsymbol{M}$ (middle). The deviation (right) of this changing magnetization can be measured as the induced signal $u(t)$ in the receive coils [20].

also be generated by a triangular function

$$\boldsymbol{H}_{AC}(t) = H_0 tri(2\pi f_0 t), \tag{2.2.2}$$

but then the particle response will be superposed by harmonics of the excitation frequency in all frequencies and a signal separation in the frequency domain becomes hard to realize [17]. Therefore, the sinusoidal excitation is mostly used.

The Langevin function

$$\mathcal{L}(\xi) = \begin{cases} (coth(\xi) - 1/\xi) & \text{when} \quad \xi \neq 0 \\ 0 & \text{when} \quad \xi = 0 \end{cases} \tag{2.2.3}$$

approximates the absolute value of the magnetization $M(\xi)$ of the nanoparticles

$$M(\xi) = c(\boldsymbol{r})m\mathcal{L}(\xi) \tag{2.2.4}$$

and can be schematically seen in figure 2.1 (left), where ξ is specified by

$$\xi = \frac{\mu_0 m ||\boldsymbol{H}(\boldsymbol{r},t)||}{k_B T} \quad \text{and} \quad m = \frac{1}{6}\pi d^3 M_s \tag{2.2.5}$$

with k_B as Boltzmann constant, T as absolute temperature, μ_0 as magnetic permeability of vacuum, M_s as saturation magnetization, and m as magnetic moment of the particles. The Langevin function models the magnetization response of the nanoparticles depending on the absolute value of the magnetic field strength $\boldsymbol{H}$, particle diameter d and temperature T. The concentration c of the nanoparticles is linearly connected with the magnetization as seen in equation 2.2.4. The nano-particles responds due to the exciting drive field with an alternating magnetization can be seen in figure 2.1 (middle). This induces a signal in the receive coils shown in figure 2.1 (right).

The non-linearity of the Langevin function is mainly depending on the diameter d of the nanoparticles. An increase of the diameter of the particle will steepen the Langevin function. The steepness of the Langevin function is an essential prerequisite for a desired high resolution. The further characteristics of the nanoparticles will be discussed in section 2.4.

2.3 Spatial encoding in MPI

Signal encoding enables the possibility to receive a signal of the nanoparticles to determine their concentration. So far one will get the signal of all nanoparticles, which are excited by the drive field. In order to allocate the signal to specific positions in the field of view, an additional selection field $\boldsymbol{H}_{DC}(\boldsymbol{r})$ has to be superposed with the drive field to

$$\boldsymbol{H}(\boldsymbol{r},t) = \boldsymbol{H}_{AC}(t) + \boldsymbol{H}_{DC}(\boldsymbol{r}) \qquad (2.3.1)$$

where $\boldsymbol{H}_{DC}(\boldsymbol{r})$ is generated by a direct current (DC).
The selection field will magnetize the nanoparticles to a saturated state. If the nanoparticles are saturated, the drive field seen in figure 2.2 (left) can no longer change the magnetization of the nanoparticles magnificently. The magnitude of the magnetization change seen in figure 2.2 (middle) becomes minimal. Therefore, the nanoparticles will induce only a fractional voltage in the receive coil depicted in figure 2.2 (right). For spatial encoding it is necessary that one

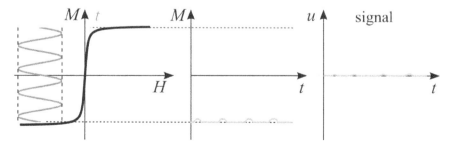

Figure 2.2: Spatial encoding: The oscillating field (left) can not excite the nanoparticles because they have been already saturated by the selection field. The magnetization (middle) does not change and no signal (right) is induced in the receive coils [20].

pcint experiences a selection field magnitude close to zero and will be able to induce a signal while the rest of the field of view is saturated by a high selection field magnitude. The point where the magnetization superposes itself to null is called field free point (FFP).

The selection field, which is also called gradient field, is shown in figure 2.3. The selection

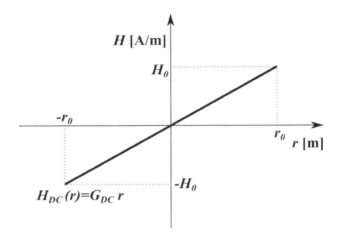

Figure 2.3: Gradient of the magnetic field $\boldsymbol{H}$.

fie d creates a linear increasing magnetic field strength from $-H_0$ to H_0 which is depending of the position r and is often written as $\boldsymbol{H}_{DC}(\boldsymbol{r}) = \boldsymbol{G}_{DC}\boldsymbol{r}$. The field free point can be found at position $r = 0$ where the magnitude of the superposed magnetization is zero. The FFP position oscillates in the range between $-\frac{H_0}{G_{DC}}$ and $\frac{H_0}{G_{DC}}$ when the overall magnetization

$$\boldsymbol{H}(\boldsymbol{r},t) = \boldsymbol{H}_{AC}(t) + \boldsymbol{H}_{DC}(\boldsymbol{r}) = H_0 sin(2\pi f_0 t) + \boldsymbol{G}_{DC}\boldsymbol{r} \qquad (2.3.2)$$

is taken into account.

In figure 2.4 the magnetization and signal chain can be seen for three different positions in the selection field. The first column shows the position related with the magnetic field strength of the selection field. In the second column the magnetization curve is shown that results from the superposed selection and drive field. The magnetization response of the nanoparticle is given in the third column and the induced voltage is shown in the fourth column.

Additionally, the fifth column presents the Fourier transformed spectrum of the signal which becomes important later when frequency space reconstruction is studied.

Through the selection field, the received signal can be allocated to the FFP position although the point is more likely a small area surrounding the FFP. The sharpness of the FFP depends on the gradient strength of the selection field and the gradient strength influences the resolution. The resolution will be discussed in section 2.6.

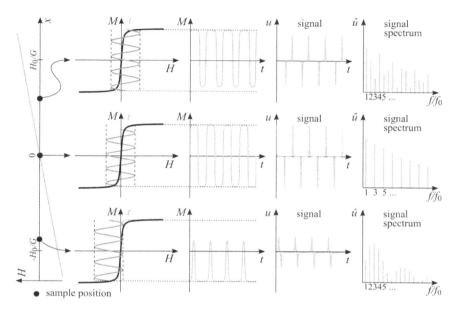

Figure 2.4: Principle of spatial encoding: The magnetization and signal chain of three different positions in the selection field are presented line by line. The position of the FFP, the magnetization curve, the resulting magnetization, the induced voltage and its spectrum are shown sequently [20].

The gradient in the selection field cannot have an arbitrary value. The magnetic flux density B has to follow the first Maxwell equation of magnetostatics 2.1.2. The divergence of the vectorfield B is null at all time. The connection between magnetic flux density and magnetic field strength is given by $B = \mu H$ where μ is a material specific permeability parameter and will be discussed further in section 2.4. This leads to the following selection field components

$$
\boldsymbol{H}_{DC}(\boldsymbol{r}) = \begin{bmatrix} 1 & 0 & 0 \\ 0 & -0.5 & 0 \\ 0 & 0 & -0.5 \end{bmatrix} \boldsymbol{r} \cdot \boldsymbol{G}_{DC}. \tag{2.3.3}
$$

where the sum of all gradient components has to be zero.

The FFP can be moved by the drive field in each spatial direction. Then, the induced signal encodes a specified position in the field of view. The gradient field is stronger in x-direction as in the MPI scanner with classical coil design which means that the possible resolution is higher in x-direction.

The small area around the FFP is then more shaped like a ellipsoid than a circle. In some cases it is advantageous to chose the same gradient strength for 2D Imaging because one wants to exclude the reason for image inhomogeneities due to different gradient strengths.

The FFP can be moved through the field of view with different trajectories and different characteristics in terms of resolution and homogeneity. One of the different trajectories namely the Lissajous trajectory will be discussed in the section 2.5.

2.4 Super-paramagnetic iron oxide nanoparticles

The super-paramagnetic iron oxide nanoparticles consist of a iron oxide core and a non-iron oxide shell surrounding the core, which is illustrated in figure 2.5. The iron oxide core is re-

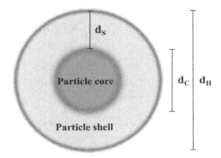

Figure 2.5: Particle model: Scheme of a super-paramagnetic iron nanoparticle with its hydrodynamic diameter d_H and its core diameter d_C and with the thickness of the shell $d_S = \frac{d_H - d_C}{2}$.

sponsible for the interaction with the magnetic field and its characteristics influence the induced signal. In order to understand why the iron oxide core, for example magnetite (Fe_3O_4), enacts super-paramagnetic and not ferromagnetic, the interaction of material with a magnetic field is discussed in detail.

There are different types of material which interact differently in a magnetic field. Some materials, for example plastic, can not be magnetised at all and will not interfere with the magnetic field in any way. Each material has a permeability value μ_r, which quantifies the degree of magnetization that a material obtains in response to an applied magnetic field. Materials such as copper, aluminium and iron, which interfere with the magnetic field, can be subdivided into the categories diamagnetism $\mu_r < 1$, paramagnetism $\mu_r > 1$ and ferromagnetism $\mu_r >> 1$. The connection between the magnetic field constant μ_0, the permeability μ_r, the magnetic field strength H and the magnetic flux density B is described in the following equations

$$\mu = \mu_r\mu_0 \qquad B = \mu H. \tag{2.4.1}$$

Diamagnetic substances like copper reduce the effect of a magnetic field and can be used as shielding against electromagnetic waves.

Paramagnetic materials such as aluminium increase the magnetic effect. The dipoles inside the material will align in the direction of the magnetic field lines, but the dipoles cannot change their position within the material and interact independent from each other. Once they are no longer exposed to a magnetic field, they will adjust themselves arbitrarily again and the magnetization vanishes.

Ferromagnetic material, such as iron, also strengthens the magnetic field lines and the dipoles will point in the direction of the magnetic field lines. But unlike paramagnetism, the dipoles can move inside the material and they interact with each other. They form domains in which the magnetic dipoles are oriented parallel.
Once the material is brought into a magnetic field, the domains grow to one large domain until the material is in saturation. When no magnetic field influences the material any more, the magnetization decrease, but not to the level it was once before. A certain rest magnetization,

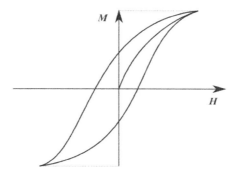

Figure 2.6: Hysteresis curve of ferromagentic objects.

which is called remanence, will still be left. The magnetization curve can be seen in figure 2.6 and describes the hysteresis of ferromagnetic substances. With this kind of hysteresis curve magnetic particle imaging would not be possible. But the nanoparticles are so small, that one particle has only one domain, which interact as one dipole.
Therefore, nanoparticles viewed together act paramagnetic, but this special form is called super-paramagnetism. The hysteresis curve looks like the Langevin function in figure 2.12(a) and the nanoparticles show no remanence any more. The size at which materials become super-

paramagnetic is at about $100\,nm$, but varies from substance to substance. The nanoparticle shell is very important for the super-paramagnetic characteristic because it inhibits the agglomeration process, which would lead to more domains again.

For different diameters the nanoparticles have a different relaxation time and they are modeled by the Brown and Néel relaxation.
The Brown and Néel relaxation describe the relaxation process of the super-paramagnetic iron oxides, when the magnetic field strength changes. Brown and Néel relaxation explain the connection between diameter of the nanoparticles and relaxation time.
The Brown relaxation models a rotation of the whole particle with core and shell in the medium. The relaxation time t_B can be calculated by

$$t_B = \frac{\eta \pi d_S^3}{2 k_B T} \qquad (2.4.2)$$

which is mainly depending on the dynamic viscosity η of the medium, the diameter d_S of the particle shell and the absolute temperature T. For particles with a shell diameter above $17\,nm$ the Brown relaxation is dominant while for shell diameters below $17\,nm$ the Néel relaxation is dominant [20].
The Néel relaxation models that the geometrical position of the particle shell stays at the same position but the magnetization in the core rotates. The relaxation time is estimated by

$$t_N = t_0 exp(\frac{K \pi d_C^3}{6 k_B T}) \qquad (2.4.3)$$

with t_0 as substance depending constant, K as magnetic anisotropy constant and d_C as core diameter. The relaxation time depends, in contrast to the Brown relaxation, on the core diameter only and is also influenced by the magnetic anisotropy factor.
The relaxation time for particles in the $[20-50]$ nm core diameter range is estimated to be in the range between $[10^{-5}-10^{-2}]$ s [20].

2.5 Lissajous trajectory

For signal encoding it is necessary, in the frequency reconstruction and x-space reconstruction, to separate between the excitation signal and the response signal. For the separation process it is advantageous that the trajectory is generated with as less frequencies as possible in the best case only one. In a multi-dimensional field of view one frequency per direction is the optimum. The sinusoidal excitation fulfills this requirement and results in the Lissajous trajectory. Although, several other trajectories fulfill this requirement of being generated by one frequency namely cartesian, spiral, radial and Lissajous trajectory, the Lissajous trajectory has proven to provide the best results in terms of homogeneity and resolution. This conclusion was drawn out from the simulation study of Knopp et al. [21], where all trajectories have been compared.

The trajectory is defined by the path $s(t)$ that the FFP follows around the field of view. In terms of the magnetic field, it can be written as

$$\boldsymbol{H}(\boldsymbol{s}(t), t) = \boldsymbol{0} \qquad t \geq 0. \tag{2.5.1}$$

The Lissajous trajectory is generated by two orthogonal harmonic oscillations with slightly different frequencies f_x and f_y. The ratio between the frequencies $\frac{f_x}{f_y} \in \mathbb{N}$ has to be formed by integers otherwise the trajectory would not be closed. In mathematical terms the 2D Lissajous trajectory can be formulated by

$$\boldsymbol{L}(t) = \begin{bmatrix} L_x(t) \\ L_y(t) \end{bmatrix} = \begin{bmatrix} A_x \sin(2\pi f_x t + \varphi_x) \\ A_y \sin(2\pi f_y t + \varphi_y) \end{bmatrix}, \qquad t \geq 0 \tag{2.5.2}$$

where A_x and A_y are the amplitudes and φ_x and φ_y the phases of the sinusoidal signals. In magnetic particle imaging, the phases are chosen to be zero ($\varphi_x = \varphi_y = 0$) because then the trajectory starts in the center of the field of view. In section 2.5.2 it is discussed how to increase the density of the Lissajous trajectory by changing the phase parameters.

In order to achieve a rational ratio

$$\frac{f_x}{f_y} = \frac{N}{N-1}, \qquad N \in \mathbb{N} \tag{2.5.3}$$

between the frequencies f_x and f_y, they are depending on a natural number N. Using N and the base frequency f_b the frequencies can be written as

$$\begin{bmatrix} f_x \\ f_y \end{bmatrix} = \begin{bmatrix} \frac{1}{N} \\ \frac{1}{N-1} \end{bmatrix} f_b. \tag{2.5.4}$$

The parameter N determines both frequencies f_x and f_y and is also a parameter for the repetition time of the Lissajous trajectory. After N periods and $N-1$ periods the oscillations L_x and L_y start again. Therefore, the repetition time is estimated by

$$T_R = \frac{N}{f_x} = \frac{N-1}{f_y} = \frac{N(N-1)}{f_b}. \tag{2.5.5}$$

If the parameter N is increased, the repetition time increases and the trajectory as a whole becomes more dense. The 2D Lissajous trajectory with different parameters $N = [2, 5, 10, 20, 32, 50]$

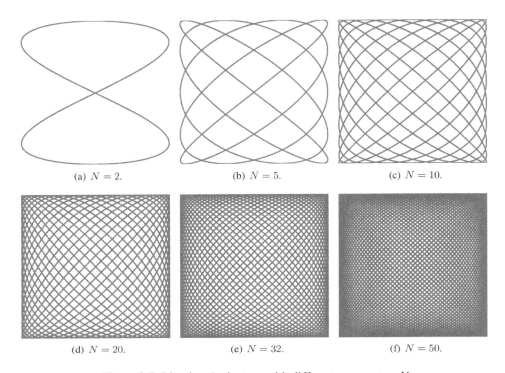

(a) $N = 2$.　　　　(b) $N = 5$.　　　　(c) $N = 10$.

(d) $N = 20$.　　　　(e) $N = 32$.　　　　(f) $N = 50$.

Figure 2.7: Lissajous trajectory with different parameters N.

is shown in figure 2.7. The disadvantage of the Lissajous trajectory is that it samples not ho-
mogeneously over the whole field of view. It is more dense at the edges and less dense in the
center, but it still represents the best results in comparison to the other trajectories [21] as stated
earlier before. Only the spiral trajectory had a great resolution in the center and could be used
in applications where only the center of the field of view is of interest.

The Lissajous trajectory can easily be extended to 3D and can be seen in figure 2.8. A third
orthogonal harmonic L_z with amplitude A_z, phase φ_z and frequency f_z is superposed with the
existing two and can be described by

$$\boldsymbol{L}(t) = \begin{bmatrix} L_x(t) \\ L_y(t) \\ L_z(t) \end{bmatrix} = \begin{bmatrix} A_x \sin(2\pi f_x t + \varphi_x) \\ A_y \sin(2\pi f_y t + \varphi_y) \\ A_z \sin(2\pi f_z t + \varphi_z) \end{bmatrix}. \tag{2.5.6}$$

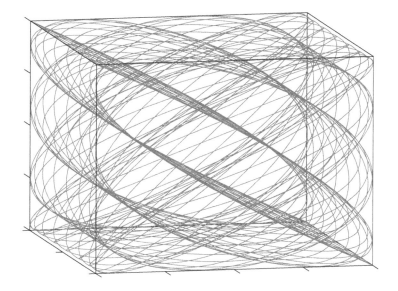

Figure 2.8: 3D Lissajous trajectory with parameter $N = 8$.

The ratio is then connected with the base frequency by

$$\begin{bmatrix} f_x \\ f_y \\ f_z \end{bmatrix} = \begin{bmatrix} \frac{1}{N} \\ \frac{1}{N-1} \\ \frac{1}{N+1} \end{bmatrix} f_b \qquad (2.5.7)$$

and for the repetition time applies

$$T_R = \frac{N(N-1)(N+1)}{f_b}. \qquad (2.5.8)$$

If the 3D Lissajous trajectory is viewed as slices in $[(x, y), (x, z), (y, z)]$ direction, the frequency ratios between each two components $[\frac{f_x}{f_y}, \frac{f_x}{f_z}, \frac{f_y}{f_z}]$ are rational again.

The formed 2D Lissajous trajectories in the $[(x, y), (x, z), (y, z)]$ direction show how dense the whole 3D trajectory is in each slice. The view of the slices can be seen in figure 2.9. The density of the Lissajous trajectory increases the resolution to a certain limit [1] but with the Lissajous trajectory it is not possible to achieve the same density in each slice.

The connection between density and repetition time will be discussed in detail for 3D in section 2.5.1.

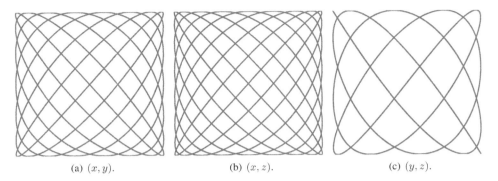

(a) (x, y).   (b) (x, z).   (c) (y, z).

Figure 2.9: 3D Lissajous trajectory with parameters $N = 8$ in slice view $[(x, y), (x, z), (y, z)]$.

2.5.1 Density and real-time condition in 3D

Magnetic particle imaging is capable of real-time imaging and for medical imaging system the real-time requirement is 25 volumes per second. That corresponds to 0.04 s per volume for one enclosed period of the Lissajous trajectory. With the condition of the excitation frequency set near 25 kHz and the real-time condition 0.04 s, the parameter N for the Lissajous trajectory for the 3D case can be derived as follows

$$3D \qquad T_R = \frac{N(N-1)(N+1)}{f_b} \qquad \text{with} \quad f_b = f_x \cdot N \qquad (2.5.9)$$

$$3D \qquad T_R = \frac{N^2 - 1}{f_x} \qquad (2.5.10)$$

$$3D \qquad N = \sqrt{T_R \cdot f_x + 1}. \qquad (2.5.11)$$

The base frequency f_b can then be calculated by

$$3D \qquad f_b = \frac{N(N-1)(N+1)}{T_R} \qquad f_{b_{factor}} = \frac{2.5\,MHz}{f_b} \qquad (2.5.12)$$

and the channel frequencies f_x, f_y, f_z are given by

$$\begin{bmatrix} f_x \\ f_y \\ f_z \end{bmatrix} = \begin{bmatrix} 2.5\,MHz/f_{b_{factor}}/N \\ 2.5\,MHz/f_{b_{factor}}/(N-1) \\ 2.5\,MHz/f_{b_{factor}}/(N+1) \end{bmatrix} \qquad (2.5.13)$$

In table 2.1 the frequencies for the drive fields in each direction are shown. The base frequency is always a fraction of $f_h = 2.5\,MHz$, because the hardware components uses this frequency.

	N	f_h	f_b	$f_{b_{factor}}$	f_x	f_y	f_z
3D	32	2.5 MHz	833.333 kHz	3	26.042 kHz	26.882 kHz	25.253 kHz

Table 2.1: The parameters for the 3D real-time condition of 25 volumes per second.

As excitation frequency $[f_x, f_y, f_z]$, so far, a frequency around 25 kHz is chosen because the particle response is satisfying at this frequency and it is above the threshold of hearing. Although 25 kHz is close to the specific absorption rate (SAR) limit when the peripheral nerve stimulation starts [22].

2.5.2 Phase shift

The presented Lissajous trajectory has the advantage that it can be generated by only one frequency. However, it has the disadvantage that once the frequency is chosen the sampling density and the repetition time are set. It is not possible to change the sampling density and the repetition time without adjusting the frequency [20].

Therefore, the resolution and frame rate are also fixed. The oscillating circuit in the hardware generating the frequency has to be calibrated very carefully and tuned to this frequency. Of course, it is possible to supply one oscillating circuit hardware for each desired frequency but that is economical not reasonable. For an application desiring an adjustable resolution and repetition time, the density of the Lissajous trajectory can be changed by using more trajectory repetition with different phases φ_x.

By this means, the resolution can be small and is traded off for the frame repetition rate. In another scenario, the frame repetition rate is increased while the resolution is sacrificed to a certain extent. But all adjustments can be made by using only one frequency hardware setup.

The trajectories seen in figure 2.10(a)-2.10(e) have all the same parameter $N = 5$ but different phases $\varphi_x = [0°, 72°, 144°, 216°, 288°]$. If the five Lissajous trajectories are superposed, they have the same density as the trajectory shown in figure 2.10(f) with parameter $N = 25$. The combined density N_{comb} of the superposed trajectory is given by

$$N_{comb} = n \cdot N_{phaseshift} \tag{2.5.14}$$

where n in the number of superposed trajectories and $N_{phaseshift}$ their density. To ensure a homogeneous combined trajectory, the phases have to be distributed equidistantly. The phases are calculated by

$$\varphi_{x,i} = 2\pi \frac{i}{n} \qquad i \in \mathbb{N} \quad i \leq n. \tag{2.5.15}$$

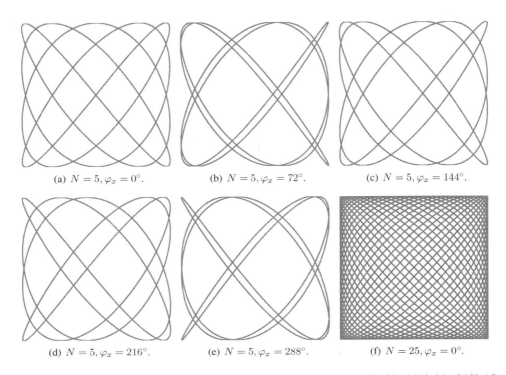

(a) $N = 5, \varphi_x = 0°$.   (b) $N = 5, \varphi_x = 72°$.   (c) $N = 5, \varphi_x = 144°$.

(d) $N = 5, \varphi_x = 216°$.   (e) $N = 5, \varphi_x = 288°$.   (f) $N = 25, \varphi_x = 0°$.

Figure 2.10: Phase shifted Lissajous trajectory with $\varphi_x = 0°$ (a), $72°$ (b), $144°$ (c), $216°$ (d), $288°$ (e), and $N = 25, 0°$ (f).

In theory, the phase shift between the trajectories is applied instantly but that is not possible in reality. The shifting time is depending on the magnitude of the shift and the used hardware. It is probably in the ms range. A huge phase shift will probably take less time then a small phase shift.

Nevertheless, the implementation of the phase shift could be useful for applications where the resolution is most important and the repetition time is negligible. For the x-space reconstruction it could also be advantageous because here the density of the Lissajous trajectory seems more important then in the frequency reconstruction. This connection will be discussed in detail in section 3.5.

The phase shift has to be analysed for 3D Lissajous trajectories but should be possible by modifying the phase in z-direction.

2.5.3 Velocity of the FFP

The velocity of the field free point is depending on the drive field. The drive field is generated by a sinusoidal oscillation with a minimal different frequency in each direction. The resulting Lissajous trajectory of the FFP is fast in the center where the sinusoidal oscillations are close to zero and slow at the edges where the sinusoidal oscillations are near one. The different veloc-

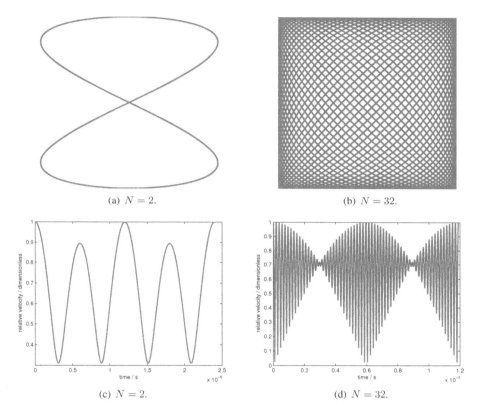

(a) $N = 2$.

(b) $N = 32$.

(c) $N = 2$.

(d) $N = 32$.

Figure 2.11: Velocity of the FFP in different Lissajous trajectories in (a) and (c) for parameter $N = 2$ and for $N = 32$ in (b) and (d).

ities in the change of the magnetization generate a different magnitude in the response signal of the magnetic particles. The faster the magnetization changes the stronger and sharper the response signal of the nanoparticles becomes.

If the magnetization changes too slowly, it is not possible to measure a signal since the measured voltage u is induced by the time derivative of the magnetic flux.

The velocity of the FFP is depicted in figure 2.11(c) and 2.11(d) for the Lisaajous trajectory with parameter $N = [2, 32]$ in figure 2.11(a) and 2.11(b).

The velocity of the FFP becomes important in the x-space reconstruction where the signal of the particles is normalized by the velocity of the FFP. It ensures that the magnitude of the particle signal is adjusted according to the FFP position. A different velocity of the FFP makes the signal either stronger or weaker.

2.6 Resolution and sensitivity in MPI

Magnetic particle imaging has, compared to other morphological imaging modalities such as PET, a high sensitivity and a high resolution [1]. Furthermore, it is able to resolve the particle concentration distribution in a 3D field of view in real-time. Real-time means that 25 volumes per second will be generated.

The theoretical resolution can be derived by the Langevin function 2.2.3 which is used for modeling the response of the nanoparticles.

The derivative of the Langevin function

$$\dot{\mathcal{L}}(\xi) = \left(\frac{1}{\xi^2} - \frac{1}{sinh^2(\xi)} \right) \tag{2.6.1}$$

with

$$\frac{d}{d\xi} M(\xi) = cm\dot{\mathcal{L}}(\xi) \tag{2.6.2}$$

defines the point spread function of the particle response [23]. As criterion for the resolution the definition that two points are resolved when both point are separated by the full-width at half-maximum is chosen. The full-width at half-maximum (FHWM) is defined as

$$f(x_1) = f(x_2) = \frac{1}{2} f(x_{max}) \tag{2.6.3}$$

and can be determined numerically as $\Delta \xi_{FHWM} \approx 4.16$ [24] from equation 2.6.1. Then the spatial resolution can be written as

$$\Delta x = \frac{k_B T}{\mu_0 m \boldsymbol{G}_{DC}} \Delta \xi_{FHWM} = \frac{6 k_B T}{\mu_0 \pi M_{sat} \boldsymbol{G}_{DC} d^3} \Delta \xi_{FHWM} \quad \text{with} \quad m = \frac{\pi}{6} d^3 M_s \tag{2.6.4}$$

and it becomes evident that the resolution is inverse proportional to the power of three $\Delta x \propto d^{-3}$ depending on the diameter of the nanoparticles. The larger the nanoparticles are, the better the resolution will improve with the power of three. But at a certain size of the nanoparticles, it was not possible to identify an improvement in the resolution [2].

The different magnetizations curves for particle diameters $[15, 20, 30, 40, 60]$ nm are illustrated in figure 2.12(a). The magnetization curve becomes steeper with increasing diameter. When the limes of the diameter is set to infinity $d \rightarrow \infty$, an ideal magnetization curve, mathematical described as step function, is yielded.

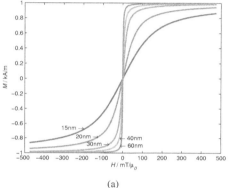 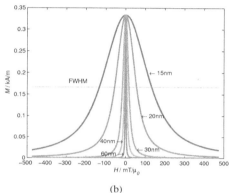

(a)   (b)

Figure 2.12: (a) Magnetization curve modeled with the Langevin function for different diameters $[15, 20, 30, 40, 60]$ nm of the nanoparticles.   (b) Derivative of the Langevin function and FWHM for different diameters $[15, 20, 30, 40, 60]$ nm of the nanoparticles.

The derivative of the magnetization curve is shown in figure 2.12(b). With increasing particle diameter the full-width at half-maximum becomes smaller and the resolution improves.

Equation 2.6.4 also clarifies that the resolution is inverse proportional $\Delta x \propto G_{DC}^{-1}$ depending on the gradient strength of the selection field. A stronger gradient will decrease the small circle or ellipsoid shaped area around the FFP and minimize the signal interference around the FFP. Therefore, the image resolution will be improved. But as one saw in section 2.5, the resolution is also significantly influenced by the choice of the trajectory and the velocity of the FFP. It is relevant at what magnitude and how fast the magnetization is changing.

Note that a strong decrease in the temperature would also increase the resolution as long as the temperature goes not below the blocking temperature because otherwise the nanoparticles would behave as ferromagnets again [23].

2.7 Signal chain for MPI

This section serves the purpose of summing up the previous presented signal steps in the MPI signal chain. The four basic equations which model the MPI signal chain are presented as follows.

At first, the **coil sensitivity** for generating p_q^G and receiving coils p_q^R is given by

$$p_q^G(r) = \frac{1}{4\pi} \int_{V_q} \frac{j_q(l) \times (r - l)}{\|r - l\|_2^3} d^3 l, \tag{2.7.1}$$

$$p_o^R(r) = \frac{1}{4\pi} \int_{V_o} \frac{j_o(l) \times (r - l)}{\|r - l\|_2^3} d^3 l, \tag{2.7.2}$$

where j_q and j_o describe the unit current density to the corresponding coils with indices q and o. V_q and V_o denote the volume to the corresponding coil. The coils sensitivities derive from equation 2.1.4, but in order to come to the magnetic field strength as presented below equation 2.4.1 and the time varying current $I_q(t)$ for each coil has to be taken into account.

Then the **magnetic field strength** is formulated as

$$H(r, t) = \sum_{q=0}^{Q-1} I_q(t) p_q^G(r) \tag{2.7.3}$$

with the number of generating coils Q, the number of receive coils O, the currents $I_q(t)$, and the currents $I_o(t)$. This equation 2.7.3 resembles the combined magnetic field strength stated in equation 2.3.2 and has been generated by the selection field and the drive field.

Furthermore, the **particle magnetization** is described by

$$M(r, t) = c(r) \overline{m}(\|H(r, t)\|_2) e_H \tag{2.7.4}$$

with the mean magnetic moment $\overline{m}$ and direction of the magnetic field e_H. This equation states the connection between the magnetic field strength, the particle properties and the particle magnetization. It was derived form equation 2.2.4.

In the end, the **induced voltage**

$$u_l(t) = -\mu_0 \int_\Omega \frac{\partial}{\partial t} M(r, t) p_o^R(r) d^3 r. \tag{2.7.5}$$

combines all previous equations and results in the voltage $u_l(t)$. The particle concentration $c(r)$ is defined in the area of Ω. The magnetic moment has been given in equation 2.2.5. The time changing particle magnetization is received as voltage in the receive coils because of the induction law presented in equation 2.1.5.

As a next step, the final voltage signal $u_l(t)$ is processed differently depending on the used reconstruction technique. So far, the signal chain for both reconstruction techniques, namely the x-space and frequency reconstruction, has been the same but now their paths split. The frequency reconstruction will be explained in section 3.3 and the x-space reconstruction will be discussed in section 3.5.

3 Methods and materials

In this chapter the different methods and materials are discussed that are relevant for this work. The simulation tool *scanner configuration* is used in this simulation study and is described in detail in section 3.1. With the help of *scanner configuration* the different scanner topologies are simulated and shown in section 3.2. The ideal scanner and the MPI scanner with classical coil setup are shortly presented. The single-sided scanner is explained in detail with its different coil geometry.

Both reconstruction methods, frequency and x-space, are explained in order to show the step from received signal to the image.

At first, the frequency reconstruction is analysed in section 3.3. It is closely examined in terms of filtering, acquiring the system function, and MPI image equation for the frequency reconstruction. Additionally, the model-based approach is presented to show an improvement of acquiring the system matrix in section 3.3.2.

Different reconstruction techniques are presented in order to solve a system of linear equations in section 3.4. The least squares problem with Tikhonov regularization, the singular value decomposition and the algebraic reconstruction technique known form CT are discussed further since they are mainly used in MPI. At the end of the frequency section, the properties of the frequency reconstruction are discussed in section 3.4.4.

Secondly, the x-space reconstruction is analysed with its differences to the frequency reconstruction in section 3.5. The x-space theory for 1D and 3D is closely examined with its MPI image equations. The practical implementation of the x-space reconstruction is presented in section 3.5.1.

For the x-space reconstruction, several deconvolution techniques are presented in section 3.5.2 in order to deconvolve the native x-space image. The Wiener deconvolution and the Tikhonov regularization are studied closely since they provide the best results so far.

As magnitude for the error of the reconstruction, the normalized root mean square deviation (NRMSD) is illustrated in end of section 3.6.

At last, the advantages and disadvantages of both reconstruction techniques are summarized and compared in section 3.6. The different aims in terms of applications is also pointed out.

3.1 Scanner configuration

The simulation tool *scanner configuration* has been especially implemented to simulate the MPI
signal and receive chain. The tool can simulate arbitrary coil types, coil sizes and coil orien-
tations. It dissembles also different nanoparticle distributions, calculates the magnetic fields,
models the nanoparticle magnetization and simulates the induced voltage in the receive coils.
Additionally, different types of noise can be added in order to make the simulation more realis-
tical. The kernel of the simulation tool has been written in C++ to ensure a fast run time. With
C++ it is also possible to program object oriented.
Hence, the simulation tool can be extended easily with new coil geometries and existing components can simply be adjusted. A graphical user inferface allows the visualization of the coil
setup and of the calculated magnetic fields. The parameters for the orientation, size, currents
and so on can be adjusted instantly.
A great advantage of this tool is that is can be used by script languages such as MATLAB©
and python. The basic simulation function of the C++ code can be called via script written in
MATLAB©. This makes the realization of huge simulation studies manageable and repeatable.

The continues equation 2.7.1, 2.7.3, 2.7.4, and 2.7.5 are discretized to evaluate them on the
computer. The discretization has to be done for the time and the location. The location discretization is realized by a cell-centered grid where the grid position is set in the middle of a
pixel or volume [25]. The time discretization is done equidistant and only the left interval limit
is considered. Further information regarding the discretization can be found in [17].
Scanner configuration is able to model circular coils, rectangle coils, saddle coils, curved rectangular coils, elliptical coils, and D-coils. Some coil types are shown in figure 3.1. The generated magnetic field depends on the location and orientation of the coil. For an easier implementation two coordinate systems are used namely the global and the coil coordinate system.
In the coil coordinate system it is assumed that the coil has a fixed orientation and lies in a fixed
plane. The coil sensitivity is then calculated in the coil coordinate system.
By this means, the calculation effort is simplified. The coil sensitivity has to be transformed to
the global coordinate system. This is realized by an affine transformation [25]

$$r = R\tilde{r} + t \tag{3.1.1}$$

where r is the position in the global coordinate system, R the 3×3 rotation matrix, $\tilde{r}$ the
position in the coil coordinate system and t the 3×1 translation vector. The coil sensitivity in

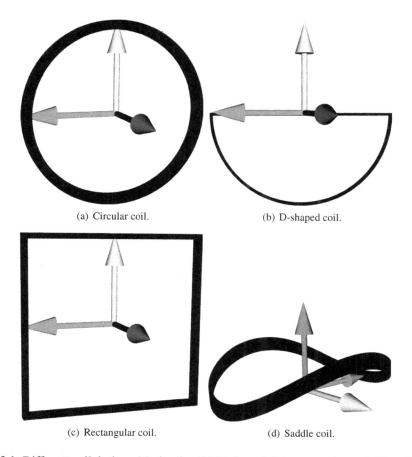

(a) Circular coil.

(b) D-shaped coil.

(c) Rectangular coil.

(d) Saddle coil.

Figure 3.1: Different coil designs (a) circular, (b) D-shaped, (c) rectangular, and (d) saddle coil.

the global coordinate system is received by solving the following equation

$$p(\boldsymbol{r}) = \boldsymbol{R}\tilde{p}(\boldsymbol{R}^{-1}(\boldsymbol{r} - \boldsymbol{t})) \tag{3.1.2}$$

where $\tilde{p}$ is the coil sensitivity in the coil coordinate system.

The coils are defined by various parameters such as inner radius, outer radius, length, windings, DC current, AC current, power loss, and many more. The parameters are different for each coil type. For the circular coils it is also helpful to define them in a cylindric coordinate system and transform them afterwards.

A detailed description of the tool *scanner configuration* can be found in [17].

3.2 Scanner topologies

The ideal scanner obtains a perfectly homogeneous magnetic field and its magnetic field is shown in figure 3.2. The ideal scanner is used to test new methods fundamentally. The gradient was chosen to be equal in both direction to avoid contortions caused by the magnetic field.

The MPI scanner with classical coil geometry shown in figure 3.3 generates a quite homoge-

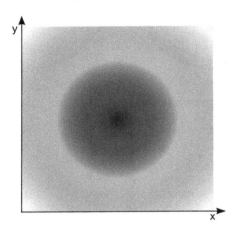

Figure 3.2: Homogeneous magnetic field of the ideal scanner.

neous magnetic field. The homogeneity decreases at the corners of the field of view although it is nearly optimal.

The selection field can be generated by two permanent magnets which are positioned with op-

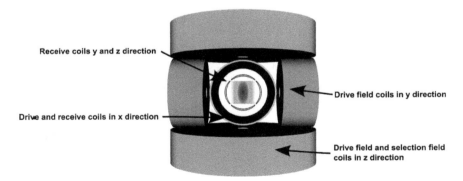

Figure 3.3: Classical coil setup for the MPI scanner.

posite magnetization towards each other. The effect is also yielded by two Maxwell coils where the currents run in opposite directions. Maxwell coils are generally used in practise.

The drive field is usually generated by to two Helmholtz coils where the currents run in parallel direction. The setup for a classical MPI scanner can be seen in figure 3.3.

The FFP has to be moved in all directions as well. Therefore, Helmholtz coil pairs for the drive field have to be added in each direction. The voltage signal is measured with three receive coils in each direction seen in figure 3.3.

The single-sided scanner is a special topology of the MPI scanner. In one scenario the single-sided scanner could be used as a hand-held device and it might be possible to apply it to a patient like an ultra sound transducer. In a MPI scanner with classical coil setup the selection field is generated by two opposing Maxwell coils of the same size. The single-sided scanner has also two opposing Maxwell coils, but one coil is smaller and it is placed inside the other one.
The modeled single-sided scanner is shown in figure 3.4. The idea for the single-sided scanner has been proposed in the original paper [1] by Gleich and Weizenecker and has been realized by Sattel et al. [10].

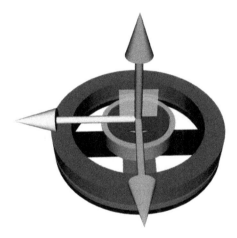

Figure 3.4: The single-sided setup simulated and visualized in *scanner configuration.*

3.3 Frequency reconstruction

In other modalities, for example x-ray computed tomography (CT) and magnetic resonance imaging (MRI) a mathematical model for the imaging process is well known. The system function, in CT for instance, is given by the geometry of the scanner.
Therefore, only data regarding the object has to be acquired and no data concerning the scanners properties or characteristics has to be gathered.

In MPI, however, the imaging process is highly connected to the variety and characteristics of the nanoparticles. The whole MPI imaging process depends on the applied magnetic fields, the FFP trajectory, the FFP velocity and the distribution of the nanoparticle size [17] [11]. In an optimized scanner these dynamics and geometries of the scanner could be generated once and then saved for further measurements. But in the research and developing process these parameters constantly change and slow down the optimization iteration.

Meanwhile, the dynamics of the scanner and the magnetic field are determined for one combination of particles and scanner setup. These properties are gathered with the system function, which will be explained in detail in the next sections 3.3.1 and 3.3.2. These sections present two approaches to obtain the system function. The first approach utilizes a measurement-based system function, while the second approach uses a model-based system function.

3.3.1 Measurement-based frequency reconstruction

In this section the necessary steps to obtain the system function are described and its connection to the particle concentration which distribution will result in the desired image.

The voltage signal that has been induced in the receive coils can be written as

$$u(t) = -\mu_0 \int_\Omega \frac{\partial}{\partial t} \overline{\boldsymbol{m}}(\boldsymbol{H}(\boldsymbol{r}, t)) \cdot \boldsymbol{p}(\boldsymbol{r}) c(\boldsymbol{r}) d^3 r \qquad (3.3.1)$$

when equations 2.7.4 and 2.7.5 are compared.

The frequency spectrum of this voltage signal $u(t)$ is used in the reconstruction process later on, but before the spectrum can be used, one additional step is necessary. The next step is the filtering on the excitation frequency.

Filtering of the excitation frequency

MPI has the property that the excitation frequency and the respond frequency of the particle are superposed. The voltage $u_l(t)$ induced in the receive coils is the sum of two partial sources the magnetization of the drive field $u_l^{drivefield}(t)$ and the magnetization of the particles $u_l^{particle}(t)$

$$u_l(t) = u_l^{drivefield}(t) + u_l^{particle}(t) \qquad (3.3.2)$$

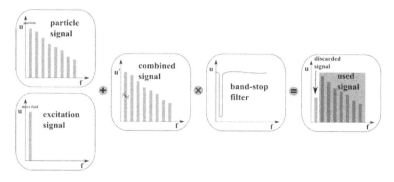

Figure 3.5: Filter chain with band-stop filter to recover the particle signal.

where l is the *l*th receiving coils in a multidimensional setup. The challenge is now to separate both signals.

First, the voltage of the excitation field $u_l^{drivefield}(t)$ with no particle in the scanner is measured. Then, the combined voltage $u_l(t)$ of both signal with particles in the scanner is measured.

In the end, the excitation field signal is subtracted from the combined signal to calculated the particle signal $u_l^{particle}(t) = u_l(t) - u_l^{drivefield}(t)$. The analogue to digital converter (ADC) is not able to transfer it directly. The best ADC has a resolution of 16 bit with sampling rates over 1 MHz, which means they can resolve in the range between $0 - 2^{16} \approx 10^5$ [17]. The excitation signal is much stronger with a magnitude of about $10^6 - 10^{10}$ depending on the particle concentration. That is why this simple approach cannot be realized.

The filtering of the excitation frequency is solved with a band-stop filter. The band-stop filter filters out the excitation signal due to its small band width. The particle signal, on the other hand, has a large band width and can be extracted from the combined signal this way. The band-stop filter is placed between the receive coil and the ADC, because the ADC has a limited dynamic range.

The information of the particle with the same frequency as the excitation frequency is discarded by the filtering but there are some approaches to recover this information [26]. The filter chain obtaining the particle signal in 1D is shown in figure 3.5. The theory of the band-stop filtering and the hardware realization can be found in [17] and [20].

Note that the signal $u(t)$ is now the filtered signal without the first harmonic.

Transformation to the frequency domain

As a next step, the filtered signal $u(t)$ is expanded into Fourier series with its coefficients

$$\hat{u}_k = \frac{1}{T} \int_0^T u(t) e^{-2\pi i \frac{kt}{T}} dt, \tag{3.3.3}$$

$$\hat{u}_k = -\mu_0 \int_\Omega \frac{1}{T} \int_0^T \frac{\partial}{\partial t} \overline{\boldsymbol{m}}(\boldsymbol{H}(\boldsymbol{r},t)) \cdot \boldsymbol{p}(\boldsymbol{r}) e^{-2\pi i \frac{kt}{T}} dt c(\boldsymbol{r}) d^3 r. \tag{3.3.4}$$

The transformation form time domain to frequency space by the Fourier transformation is illustrated schematically in figure 3.6. As mentioned before, the first harmonic namely the excitation

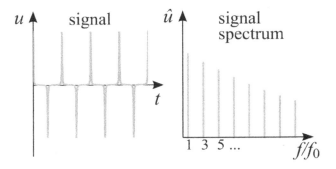

Figure 3.6: Transformation of the signal to Fourier space [27].

frequency is filtered out. Additionally, the higher harmonics, which are below the noise level, are left out in the spectrum. They are left out because they introduce only noise and contain no further useful information. Note that for the reconstruction it is not necessary to gain the whole spectrum. As one will see in section 3.3.3, the linear system of equation needs to be only invertible in order to reconstructed the distribution of the nanoparticles. But the more harmonics are recovered, the better the reconstructed image will get in the end.

Acquiring the system function

For obtaining the system function $\hat{s}_k(\boldsymbol{r})$ a delta sample of precise concentration and size is chosen. For each position $\boldsymbol{r}_n$ of the delta sample, the induced voltage $u^n(t)$ is measured and their Fourier coefficients $\hat{u}_k^n$ are calculated. A set of frequency components $\hat{u}_k^n$ is generated when the probe position is shifted through positions $\boldsymbol{r}_n$, $n = 0, ..., N-1$. With the set of frequency components $\hat{u}_k^n$ the system function is determined and filled column by column with the frequency components [11].

The system function can be estimated by the acquired frequency components by setting

$$\hat{s}_k(\boldsymbol{r}_n) \approx \frac{\hat{u}_k^n}{c_0 \Delta V} \tag{3.3.5}$$

for each position $\boldsymbol{r}_n$ and where c_0 is the known concentration of the delta sample and ΔV is the volume of the sample. This estimation can only be done, if the size of the sample is less than or equal to the voxel size of the sampled grid. If the size of the sample is larger than the voxel, the connection between the frequency components and the concentration is given by the convolution

$$\hat{u}_k^n = \int_\Omega \hat{s}_k(\boldsymbol{r}_n) K(\boldsymbol{r} - \boldsymbol{r}_n) d^3 r \tag{3.3.6}$$

where K is the convolution kernel. With a given kernel the system function can be restored by a deconvolution. Since the deconvolution is an ill-posed problem, the deconvolution needs a small kernel size compared to the field of view in order to be successful. In practise, the deconvolution was not applied, because the noise level was also too high and a sample size of about the same size as the voxel was advised by [10], [9].

To sum up, the choice of the sample size needs to be balanced between the signal-to-noise ratio and the desired resolution. In order to avoid noise and increase the resolution, the idea of a model-based system function was proposed and performed by Knopp et al. [11], [12] and will be presented in section 3.3.2.

MPI image equation for the frequency reconstruction

The MPI image equation for the frequency reconstruction is a linear connection between the particle concentration $c(\boldsymbol{r})$ and the Fourier coefficients $\hat{u}_k$ in relation to the system function. This connection is given by the linear integral equation

$$\hat{u}_k = \int_\Omega \hat{s}_k(\boldsymbol{r}) c(\boldsymbol{r}) d^3 r \tag{3.3.7}$$

where $\hat{s}_k(\boldsymbol{r})$ is the system function and Ω denotes the volume of the FOV. The system function $\hat{s}_k(\boldsymbol{r})$ has been obtained with a delta sample of precise concentration and size as mentioned before. The filtered signal spectrum $\hat{u}_k$ has been measured for an unknown particle concentration $c(\boldsymbol{r})$. The unknown particle concentration $c(\boldsymbol{r})$ contains the actual image information. In order to receive this image information the continues MPI image equation has to be discretized, which will be presented in section 3.3.3, and the linear system of equation needs to be inverted.

For the inversion of the system matrix three algorithms will be presented in section 3.4.

If the system function is measured, it also contains the characteristics of the magnetic field and scanner with its magnetic field properties, but the acquisition time is very long.
Therefore, the idea of a model-based system function was advanced by Knopp et al. [11], [12].

3.3.2 Model-based system function

The model-based reconstruction is based on the equations modeling the physics, which are presented in section 2.7. In general, the excitation frequency is suppressed by a band-stop filter, which is applied to the recording coil while receiving the signal. If the system function is measured, the band-stop filtering is realized through hardware components with its internal transfer function a_k, but for the model-based system function is has to be estimated or measured once.
Then the signal can be modeled in the frequency domain by

$$\hat{u}_k = -\mu_0 \int_\Omega \left(\frac{a_k}{T} \int_0^T \frac{\partial}{\partial t} \widehat{\boldsymbol{M}}(\boldsymbol{r},t) \cdot \boldsymbol{p}(\boldsymbol{r}) e^{-2\pi i \frac{kt}{T}} dt \right) c(\boldsymbol{r}) d^3 r \qquad (3.3.8)$$

where the complex factor a_k denotes the transfer function of the analog receive chain and $\widehat{\boldsymbol{M}}(\boldsymbol{r},t)$ is the magnetization at unit concentration.
The model-based system function is then defined by

$$\hat{s}_k^{model} = \frac{a_k}{T} \int_0^T \frac{\partial}{\partial t} \widehat{\boldsymbol{M}}(\boldsymbol{r},t) \cdot \boldsymbol{p}(\boldsymbol{r}) e^{-2\pi i \frac{kt}{T}} dt. \qquad (3.3.9)$$

If the unit magnetization $\widehat{\boldsymbol{M}}(\boldsymbol{r},t)$ and the sensitivity profile $\boldsymbol{p}(\boldsymbol{r})$ of the receive coils are given, the system function can be set up instantly at any given position.
For the transfer function a_k of the receive chain, sampled values of the measured based system function have to be used to approximate the model-based system function better to the measured based system function. This optimization process is done by a linear regression. The function

$$f(a_k) = \int_\Omega \left| \hat{s}_k^{meas}(\boldsymbol{r}) - a_k \tilde{s}_k^{model}(\boldsymbol{r}) \right|^2 d^3 r \qquad (3.3.10)$$

calculated for each frequency index k has be minimized in order to get the complex values. The system function components $\tilde{s}_k^{model} = \frac{\hat{s}_k^{model}}{a_k}$ denotes the model-based system function with the unit transfer function and $\hat{s}_k^{meas}(\boldsymbol{r})$ describes the measurement-based system function.

The minimization condition is solved by computing the following equation

$$a_k = \frac{\int_\Omega \hat{s}_k^{meas}(\boldsymbol{r}) \overline{\tilde{s}_k^{model}(\boldsymbol{r})} d^3r}{\int_\Omega \left| \tilde{s}_k^{model}(\boldsymbol{r}) \right|^2 d^3r} \tag{3.3.11}$$

In general, the values of a_k can be computed by a single spatial position that has been measured. The number of measurement scans is usually higher, but the number of measurements required to optimize the model-based system function has to be significantly smaller than real total number of measurements for the measurement-based system function. Otherwise, the time saving would become obsolete.

To sum up, the model-based system function needs parameters about the magnetic field vector at all position at each time point. The currents generating this static selection field as well as the drive field have to be known. The frequencies of the excitation currents and their amplitudes need to be given.
Further, the magnetization curve as the Langevin function is calculated although it might not represent the correct distribution of the particle sizes. The transfer function is again optimized by using a linear regression on previous measurement-based scans.

Knopp et al. [12] stated that the results of the measurement-based system function were better than model-based system function for the bounds of the 2D image. For the center part the model-based system function achieved satisfying results, but the image quality of the measurement-based system function could not be matched. The reason for these difference could be in the geometrical displacements at the field of view bounds, which are better reproduced in the measurement-based system function. As further reasons the imperfection of of the coil geometry and the existing eddy currents could be found. The particle diameter, however, seem to have a minor influence on the model-based system function. The main reason is identified in the anisotropy of the magnetic nanoparticles, which was not modeled in this approach.

Note that in 1D, the system function for ideal particles is given by the Chebychev polynoms. For real particles the system function can be described as a convolution of the Chebyshev polynoms with the average magnetic moment to the field strength [24], [17].

In conclusion, the model-based system function has several useful advantage that come along with some drawbacks. The model-based system function can be discretized to an arbitrary small grid. The long acquisition time is shortened extremely and the memory storage is minimized. The noise level is reduced by the model-based approach, but since the model of the magnetization of the particle is still not precise enough the model-based system function cannot achieve the desired resolution.

3.3.3 System matrix

The continuous integral equation has to be discretized in order to solve it. The integral is approximated by a sum over all spatial points n. This is done by the following signal equation

$$\hat{u}_{l,k} \approx \Delta V \sum_{n=0}^{N-1} \hat{s}_{k,l}(\boldsymbol{r}_n) c(\boldsymbol{r}_n). \tag{3.3.12}$$

The signal equation is set up for every receive channel l depending on the dimensions the measurement is done. Shortly, the signal equation is written

$$\hat{\boldsymbol{S}}_l \boldsymbol{c} = \hat{\boldsymbol{u}}_l \qquad \text{with} \quad l = 1, 2, 3 \tag{3.3.13}$$

where $\hat{\boldsymbol{S}}_l$ is a $K \times N$ matrix with N columns for each spatial position the delta sample has been positioned. K denotes the number of frequency components and the system matrix consists of complex values. The vector $K \times 1$ $\hat{\boldsymbol{u}}_l$ contains the frequency components for the actual measurements with unknown particle concentration $c(\boldsymbol{r})$ at $N \times 1$ spatial positions. The particle concentration vector only consists of real values $\mathbb{R}$. Mathematically written, the definitions are given by

$$\hat{\boldsymbol{S}}_l = \Delta V \hat{S}_{l,k}(\boldsymbol{r}_n)_{k=0,\dots,K-1}^{n=0,\dots,N-1} \in \mathbb{C} \qquad \hat{\boldsymbol{u}}_l = (\hat{u}_{l,k})_{k=0}^{K-1} \in \mathbb{C} \qquad c = (c(\boldsymbol{r}_n))_{n=0}^{N-1} \in \mathbb{R}. \tag{3.3.14}$$

The system matrices for each receive channel can be combined to one large system of linear equations

$$\hat{\boldsymbol{S}} \boldsymbol{c} = \hat{\boldsymbol{u}} \tag{3.3.15}$$

where $\hat{\boldsymbol{S}}$ has the dimension $M \times N$ with $M = l \cdot K$.

This system of linear equation has to be solved in order to reconstruct the image given by the particle concentration distribution. Solving a linear system is a common problem and there are several mathematical algorithms available dealing with this problem. The singular value decomposition, the Kaczmarz algorithm and least squares problem with Tikhonov regularization, which are most commonly used for MPI, are presented in the next section.

3.4 Reconstruction techniques for solving the system of equations

In this section, the least squares problem with Tikhonov regularization is presented with its advantages and disadvantages. The singular value decomposition is analysed as the mighty tool to solve linear equation system as direct problem. The Karczmarz algorithm is studied as one of the iterative techniques and has proven to achieve the most promising results for MPI so far [17].

For solving this inverse problem

$$\hat{S}c = \hat{u}, \tag{3.4.1}$$

several assumptions have to be made. The measurement $\hat{u}$ of the desired particle distribution is also superposed with thermal noise, additionally added in the receive coils. With noise $\hat{\eta}$ the equation system looks like the following

$$\hat{S}c \approx \hat{u} + \hat{n}. \tag{3.4.2}$$

The noise challenges the reconstruction technique since it converts the problem into an ill-posed problem. An ill-posed problem is given if one characteristic of the opposite well-posed problem is not given. A well-posed problem is defined by Hadamard [28] with three requirements. These requirements are

1. existence: A solution for this equation system exists,

2. uniqueness: The problem has only one solution,

3. stability: The solution hardly changes, when the initial conditions are slightly changed.

For discrete well-posed problem the last condition means that the system matrix has to have a good condition. The condition depends on the condition number $\kappa(\hat{S})$, which is calculated by

$$\kappa(\hat{S}) = \frac{s_{max}(\hat{S})}{s_{min}(\hat{S})}, \tag{3.4.3}$$

where $s_{max}(\hat{S})$ and $s_{min}(\hat{S})$ denote the maximum singular and the minimum singular value of the system matrix. The singular value decomposition with its singular values will be explained in section 3.4.2.

3.4.1 Least squares problem with Tikhonov regularization

The presented system of linear equations is an ill-posed problem and therefore the system has to be extended with a regularization term [29], [30]. The normal least squares problem is extended by the regularization term $\lambda \, ||c||_2^2$. The regularization term is used to avoid solutions where the Euclid Norm becomes very high. This is usually the case when the solution is adjusted to the noise. In general, all regularization methods approximate the original system of linear equation with a similar version in order to achieve a well-posed problem. With an adequate choice of the parameter λ the residuum can be minimized to the noise level. The least squares problem

$$\left|\left|\hat{S}c - (\hat{u} + \hat{\eta})\right|\right|_2^2 + \lambda \, ||c||_2^2 \to \min \tag{3.4.4}$$

is normally solved by a weighted normal equation systems of first order. The weighted normal equation systems of first order

$$(\hat{S}^H W \hat{S} + \lambda I)c = \hat{S}^H W \tilde{u} \tag{3.4.5}$$

has one solution c_λ^W for $\lambda > 0$ where the matrix $(\hat{S}^H W \hat{S} + \lambda I)$ has a quadratic form. The signal and the noise are combined to $\tilde{u} = \hat{u} + \hat{\eta}$. The matrix $W = diag((w_j)_{j=0}^{M-1})$ denotes the weighted matrix that is used for inconsistent system.

Normally, in a consistent system the multiplication of each row with a positive factor does not change the solution. In inconsistent systems, however, this is not the case and the system is weighted especially when it is not equidistant discretized.

In the end, a compromise between the extent of the approximation and the condition of the system has to be found.

The choice of the regularization parameter λ can be done manually by visible inspection of the result or by automated estimation through the L-curve method. The L-curve method plots the square of the residuum norm $\left|\left|\hat{S}c_\lambda^W - \tilde{u}\right|\right|_2^2$ and the square of the solution norm $||c_\lambda^W||_2^2$ logarithmically. The curve usually looks like a L-curve depending on the regularization parameter λ. The best choice for λ can be found in the corner of the L-curve. It resembles the best balance between the residuum norm and the solution norm. The method is known to be robust with only a few exceptions [31].

3.4.2 Singular value decomposition

The singular value decomposition (SVD) is a powerful tool to classify and solve ill-posed inverse problems. The SVD can also be used as an regularization technique by using the decomposition efficiently for these purposes. The computation of the decomposition is time and memory storage consuming. The base vectors also have to be stored in order to perform the decomposition and cannot be calculated instantly [32].
Due to these challenging characteristics more efficient techniques are preferred, but the SVD can provide a solid and stable solution.

To solve the system of linear equations $\hat{S}c = \tilde{u}$ the system matrix $\hat{S} \in \mathbb{C}^{M \times N}$ is decomposed in three parts

$$\hat{S} = U \Sigma V^H \tag{3.4.6}$$

where

$$U \in \mathbb{C}^{M \times P} \quad \text{and} \quad V \in \mathbb{C}^{N \times P} \tag{3.4.7}$$

are orthogonal, complex matrices also called unitary matrices. Unitary matrices have the characteristic that their inverse matrix is equal to conjugate transposed also Hermitian transposed matrix

$$U^{-1} = U^* = U^H. \tag{3.4.8}$$

The diagonal matrix

$$\Sigma = diag(s) \in \mathbb{R}^{P \times P} \tag{3.4.9}$$

consists of the singular values $s_i = (s_0, ..., s_{P-1})^T$ which are sorted in decreasing order $s_0 > s_1 > ... > s_{P-1}$. The solution $c = \hat{S}^{-1} \tilde{u}$ for the inverse system matrix can then be calculated as follows

$$\hat{S}^{-1} = (U \Sigma V^H)^{-1} \tag{3.4.10}$$

$$\hat{S}^{-1} = (V^H)^{-1}(U \Sigma)^{-1} \tag{3.4.11}$$

$$\hat{S}^{-1} = V \Sigma^{-1} U^{-1} \tag{3.4.12}$$

$$\hat{S}^{-1} = V \Sigma^{-1} U^H \tag{3.4.13}$$

The solution of the least squares problem in equation 3.4.4 can explicitly calculated by the SVD, here written as a sum

$$c^W = \sum_{i=0}^{P-1} \frac{U_{.,i}^H \tilde{u}}{s_i} V_{.,i} \tag{3.4.14}$$

with ith column of $U_{.,i}$ and the ith column of $V_{.,i}$. With the help of the smallest and biggest singular value the condition number is estimated in equation 3.4.3. If the smallest singular value becomes very small, the condition number increases rapidly and the noise is amplified. In order to prevent this from happening, the singular values are cut off at a certain threshold. The small singular values are responsible for an unstable solution and have to be above the noise level.

The first regularization method cuts off the singular values at index p to ensure that the fraction $\frac{s_c}{s_r}$ stays small. This technique is called truncated singular value decomposition (TSVD) and the index p functions as regularization parameter.

The second method uses a filter factor

$$y_i := \frac{s_i^2}{s_i^2 + \lambda} \tag{3.4.15}$$

in the sum

$$c^W = \sum_{i=0}^{P-1} y_i \frac{U_{.,i}^H \tilde{u}}{s_i} V_{.,i} \tag{3.4.16}$$

and attenuates the solution for small singular values. High singular values are not influenced since $y_i \approx 1$ becomes close to 1, if the singular values are significant higher than $s_i >> \lambda$.

3.4.3 Kaczmarz algorithm

The Kaczmarz algorithm is an example for an iterative splitting method [33] and has proven to provide efficient results for the MPI system matrix [17]. The Kaczmarz technique is a well studied application in computed tomography (CT) where it is known as algebraic reconstruction techniques (ART) [34]. ART has become even more important in CT compared to the filtered backprojection because it provides more accurate results and modern computer hardware has made it possible to perform it on the scanner hardware.

The Kaczmarz algorithm can solve arbitrary $M \times N$ matrices in contrast to other splitting techniques such as the Gauß-Seidel-, and the Jacobi-technique that need the matrix to be quadratic [17].

The Kaczmarz algorithm rests on a fix point iteration

$$c^{l+1} = c^l + \frac{\tilde{u}_l - \left\langle \hat{S}_j^*, c^l \right\rangle}{\left\| \hat{S}_l \right\|_2^2} \hat{S}_l^*$$ (3.4.17)

where l denotes the index of the inner iteration and j describes the index of the row that is usually given in the form $j = l \; mod \; M$. The initialization is done by a null vector. The algorithm iterates then through all matrix rows.

The classical Kaczmarz iteration cannot be applied to least squares problem because the system matrix is not consistent and has to be adjusted by a diagonal weighting matrix. The Kaczmarz algorithm solves the adjusted system

$$\left[W^{\frac{1}{2}} \hat{S} \quad \lambda I \right] \begin{bmatrix} c \\ v \end{bmatrix} = W^{\frac{1}{2}} \tilde{u}$$ (3.4.18)

that represents the regularized least squares problem. The introduced vector $v = \frac{1}{\lambda} W^{\frac{1}{2}} (\hat{S} c - \tilde{u})$ denotes the weighted residuum vector, which becomes clear when the matrix-vector multiplication is solved with equation 3.4.18.

The algorithm works especially well, if the system matrix is nearly orthogonal. It was shown in [35], [36], [37] that the convergence velocity was very slow for almost linear dependent rows compared to a nearly orthogonal matrix.

The time complexity of one iteration is $\mathcal{O}(M \cdot N)$ and it is the same as one iteration of the conjugate gradient method (CGNR), which will not be discussed in this work. The results of Knopp et al. show that the Kaczmarz algorithm provided the best results in terms of reconstruction time, precision, and storage efficiency [17].

3.4.4 Properties and discussion of the frequency reconstruction

The system function is generated by shifting a small 3D volume delta sample with known size and concentration through the field of view. The measured response of each delta sample position is used to form the system matrix. The system matrix maps the particle distribution and concentration to the induced voltage in the receive coils. Since it is measured, it regards the inhomogeneous magnetic field and characteristics of the particles. This method has proven to obtain good results in the reconstruction [10], [9]. As mentioned before, the acquiring of the system function has several disadvantages.

These drawbacks are

- one system function for one combination of particles and scanner setup,

- long acquisition time, especially for 3D,

- memory demanding,

- runtime intensive solution of a linear equation system.

The long acquisition time occurs because the delta sample has to be moved to all spatial position in the field of view. The movement is done by a robot. If one assumes that it takes one second for measuring and moving the sample form one position to the next, a 3D field of view discretized in $64 \times 64 \times 64$ positions takes about 72 hours to calibrate [20].
In recently published results, the 3D field of view was limited to $32 \times 20 \times 28$ due to this reason. The acquisition time here is still 5 hours [20]. While measuring the system matrix, noise is introduced through the sample. A small delta sample is used to ensure a high resolution in the later reconstructed image. But a reduction of the sample leads to a smaller signal and that means a worse signal-to-noise ratio (SNR).
Therefore, the size of the sample can only be reduced so far as long as the SNR becomes not too small. The system matrix request a lot of memory on the hard drive since every single entry has to be saved. For the solution of the linear system of equations the system matrix has to be loaded in the random access memory (RAM) at once. Modern hardware is capable of doing so, but it is expensive and the runtime for solving the equation system is also enormous.
The model-based system matrix has improved the acquisition time, but this approach was not able to yield the same image quality and resolution as the measurement-based approach.

Meanwhile, Goodwill et al. [23], [26] have presented a reconstruction technique that does not require the system function. But their x-space reconstruction has also some drawbacks and certain requirements. The details of the x-space reconstruction will be discussed in the section 3.5 together with a comparison of advantages and disadvantages for both techniques in section 3.6.

3.5 X-space reconstruction

The x-space theory has been proposed and carried out by Goodwill et al. [23], [26] and assumes the same characteristics and methods, as the previously presented, expect for the reconstruction. It assumes the same theory for the particle magnetization in terms of the Langevin function and it also uses a selection field for spatial encoding and a drive field for signal encoding. As trajectory Goodwill et al. used a Cartesian trajectory instead of the Lissajous trajectory, because it is easier to regrid.

X-space theory in 1D

In general, x-space MPI acknowledges the imaging process as linear and describes it as a convolution. As scanner setup the MPI scanner with classical coil design presented in figure 3.3 is utilized. It has a convenient linear gradient $\boldsymbol{G}_{DC}$ and an time-changing selection field $\boldsymbol{H}_{AC}(t)$ as shown in the previous section 2.3 and in figure 2.3.

The FFP position in the one-dimensional case can then be described by

$$x_s(t) = \boldsymbol{G}_{DC}^{-1} \boldsymbol{H}_{AC}(t) \tag{3.5.1}$$

when comparing equation 2.3.2 and 2.5.1. The equation 3.5.1 is substituted into 2.3.2 and yields to the following equation

$$\boldsymbol{H}(x,t) = \boldsymbol{G}_{DC}(x_s(t) - x). \tag{3.5.2}$$

The magnetization curve M of the magnetic nanoparticles has been described earlier in section 2.2 and states the equation 2.2.4. The equation 3.5.2 is then inserted into the Langevin function 2.2.3 and results in the connection

$$M(x,t) = mc(x)\mathcal{L}[k(\boldsymbol{G}_{DC}(x_s(t) - x)] \qquad \text{with} \qquad k = \frac{\mu_0 m}{k_B T}. \tag{3.5.3}$$

With the help of the sensitivity p of the receive coil, the one-dimensional magnetization is converted into a flux density Φ [23] and the magnetization density changes only along x. The resulting convolution

$$\Phi(t) = -pm \int c(x)\mathcal{L}[\boldsymbol{G}_{DC}(x_s(t) - x)]dx \tag{3.5.4}$$

$$= -pmc(x) * \mathcal{L}[k\boldsymbol{G}_{DC}x] \tag{3.5.5}$$

describes a system where the magnetic particle density is convolved with the Langevin function kernel. In general, it is assumed that the magnetic nanoparticles do not have an influence on the magnetic field $\boldsymbol{H}$. The deviation of the magnetic flux density $\Phi(t)$ reveals the voltage that is measured in the receive coils. Then the signal in volts is given by

$$u(t) = -\frac{d}{dt}pm \int c(x)\mathcal{L}[k\boldsymbol{G}_{DC}(x_s(t) - x)]dx \qquad (3.5.6)$$

$$u(t) = pm \int c(x)\dot{\mathcal{L}}[k\boldsymbol{G}_{DC}(x_s(t) - x)] \cdot k\boldsymbol{G}_{DC}\dot{x}_s(t)dx \qquad (3.5.7)$$

$$u(t) = pmc(x) * \dot{\mathcal{L}}[k\boldsymbol{G}_{DC}x] \cdot k\boldsymbol{G}_{DC}\dot{x}_s(t) \qquad (3.5.8)$$

and forms the 1D MPI signal equation of x-space theory [14]. The velocity of the FFP is given by $\dot{x}_s(t)$ and the point spread function in form of the derivative of the Langevin function $\dot{\mathcal{L}}$ 2.6.1 has been discussed in section 2.6 and is strongly connected with the resolution.

X-space MPI image equation in 1D

By shifting the equation 3.5.8, the reconstruction equation for the image can be written as

$$Img(x(t)) = \frac{u(t)}{pmk\boldsymbol{G}_{DC}\dot{x}_s(t)} = c(x) * \dot{\mathcal{L}}[k\boldsymbol{G}_{DC}x]. \qquad (3.5.9)$$

This connection implies that under certain circumstances MPI is a linear, space invariant (LSI) system. The equation basically states that the receive signal $u(t)$ is divided by various constants and the velocity of the field free point. The value is then written to the position of the FFP at the specific time point. In order to obtain the nanoparticle concentration distribution $c(x)$, the received image also known as the native image has to be deconvolved with the derivative of the Langevin function. This assumes that the PSF is invariant for the whole field of view and that the magnetic field is homogeneous to ensure this characteristic.

X-space MPI imaging needs several requirements to formulate the image reconstruction as presented. These requirements are a high gradient to ensure a homogeneous magnetic field and a small field of view for an invariant PSF. Otherwise it would not be possible to describe the image Img as a convolution between the concentration $c(x)$ and the PSF $\dot{\mathcal{L}}[k\boldsymbol{G}_{DC}x]$. Nevertheless, a system function with a long acquisition time and solving a linear system of equations are not necessary.

For 1D the x-space formulation is exact and the reconstruction can be done by a well-behaved quasi-Lorentzian point spread function. The imaging process is linear and it is described by a convolution. For a three-dimensional setup the reconstruction becomes more challenging and the theory is not as exact as for 1D [23].

X-space MPI theory in 3D

For 3D the gradient field is assumed as in equation 2.3.3 and is given by

$$\boldsymbol{H}(\boldsymbol{r},t) = \boldsymbol{H}_{AC}(t) - \boldsymbol{G}_{DC}\boldsymbol{r} \qquad (3.5.10)$$

with the difference that the gradient $\boldsymbol{G}_{DC}$ is now a 3×3 matrix and the position $\boldsymbol{r} = [x, y, z]'$ is now a 3×1 vector. Again, the magnetic field is solved for the FFP position $\boldsymbol{r}_s(t)$ and the magnetic field coordinate $\boldsymbol{r}$ that can be written as

$$\boldsymbol{H}(\boldsymbol{r},t) = \boldsymbol{G}_{DC}(\boldsymbol{r}_s(t) - \boldsymbol{r}). \qquad (3.5.11)$$

The gradient $\boldsymbol{G}_{DC}$ needs to be invertible which is given by ideal gradients along x, y, and z axis. The magnetization curve in form of the Langevin function has to be extended by the direction of the magnetization of the nanoparticles. The magnetization in then given by

$$\boldsymbol{M}(\boldsymbol{H}(\boldsymbol{r},t)) = mc(\boldsymbol{r})\mathcal{L}[k\,||\boldsymbol{H}(\boldsymbol{r},t)||]\frac{\boldsymbol{H}(\boldsymbol{r},t)}{||\boldsymbol{H}(\boldsymbol{r},t)||_2} \qquad (3.5.12)$$

and by substituting equation 3.5.11 the magnetization is described by

$$\boldsymbol{M}(\boldsymbol{H}(\boldsymbol{r},t)) = mc(\boldsymbol{r})\mathcal{L}[k\,||\boldsymbol{G}_{DC}(\boldsymbol{r}_s(t) - \boldsymbol{r})||]\frac{\boldsymbol{G}_{DC}(\boldsymbol{r}_s(t) - \boldsymbol{r})}{||\boldsymbol{G}_{DC}(\boldsymbol{r}_s(t) - \boldsymbol{r})||_2}. \qquad (3.5.13)$$

The signal in the receive coils is determined by using the reciprocity and needs the sensitivity of the receive coils in three dimensions. The sensitivity $-\boldsymbol{p}(\boldsymbol{r})$ is a diagonal 3×3 matrix and denotes the sensitivities in the axes. Then the signal $u(t)$ is calculated, comparing equation 3.3.1, by

$$u(t) = \frac{d}{dt}\int \boldsymbol{p}(\boldsymbol{r})\boldsymbol{M}(\boldsymbol{H}(\boldsymbol{r},t))d^3r. \qquad (3.5.14)$$

The general MPI x-space signal equation is derived by applying the differential operator $\frac{d}{dt}$ and the detailed steps are presented in [23], [14]. It results in

$$u(t) = \boldsymbol{p}(\boldsymbol{r})mc(\boldsymbol{r}) * * * k\left|\left|\dot{\boldsymbol{r}}_s(t)\right|\right|h(\boldsymbol{r})\breve{\boldsymbol{r}}_s \qquad (3.5.15)$$

with

$$\breve{\boldsymbol{r}}_s = \frac{\dot{\boldsymbol{r}}}{||\boldsymbol{r}||} - \frac{\dot{\boldsymbol{r}}^T\boldsymbol{r}}{||\boldsymbol{r}||^3}\boldsymbol{r}, \qquad (3.5.16)$$

where the point spread function (PSF) can be described by the following equation

$$h(\boldsymbol{r}) = \dot{\mathcal{L}}[k\,||\boldsymbol{G}_{DC}\boldsymbol{r}||]\frac{\boldsymbol{G}_{DC}\boldsymbol{r}}{||\boldsymbol{G}_{DC}\boldsymbol{r}||}(\frac{\boldsymbol{G}_{DC}\boldsymbol{r}}{||\boldsymbol{G}_{DC}\boldsymbol{r}||})^T\boldsymbol{G}_{DC} + \frac{\mathcal{L}[k\,||\boldsymbol{G}_{DC}\boldsymbol{r}||]}{[k\,||\boldsymbol{G}_{DC}\boldsymbol{r}||]} \cdot ... \qquad (3.5.17)$$

$$\left(\boldsymbol{I} - \frac{\boldsymbol{G}_{DC}\boldsymbol{r}}{||\boldsymbol{G}_{DC}\boldsymbol{r}||}(\frac{\boldsymbol{G}_{DC}\boldsymbol{r}}{||\boldsymbol{G}_{DC}\boldsymbol{r}||})^T\right)\boldsymbol{G}_{DC}. \qquad (3.5.18)$$

X-space MPI image equation in 3D

The general x-space MPI image equation expresses the transformation from the time domain to the image domain. This is done by gridding the sampled receive signal $u(t)$ to a real space, or x-space grid, that correspondes to the instantaneous location of the FFP. The gerenal x-space image equation is then formulated by

$$Img(\boldsymbol{r}_s(t)) = \frac{u(t) \cdot \tilde{\boldsymbol{\dot{r}}}_s}{\boldsymbol{p}(\boldsymbol{r})m\,||\dot{\boldsymbol{r}}_s(t)||} = c(\boldsymbol{r}) * * * \tilde{\boldsymbol{\dot{r}}}_s \cdot h(\boldsymbol{r})\tilde{\boldsymbol{\dot{r}}}_s. \qquad (3.5.19)$$

The signal is normalized by the magnitude of the FFP velocity and the image equation is similar to the k-space analysis of MRI [14] but in MPI the scanning is done in x-space and not in k-space. That makes a Fourier transformation unnecessary. The native image in x-space has to be deconvolved with the PSF in order to obtain the actual image.

How the x-space reconstruction theory is implemented in practise, is presented in the next section 3.5.1. The following section 3.5.2 gives detailed information about the deconvolution of the blurred native image with the point spread function.

3.5.1 Implementation of the x-space reconstruction

The implemented x-space reconstruction algorithm can be divided into four parts. These parts are

1. Superpose channel signals to one signal

2. Normalize superposed signal with velocity of the FFP

3. Grid the signal from the time domain to the image domain

4. Deconvolve the image with the PSF.

The single steps of the reconstruction algorithm are illustrated in a simple example using the basic Lissajous trajectory. The phantom and the path of the Lissajous trajectory are shown in figure 3.7. The induced signal in volts is received in two channels $u_x(t_i)$ and $u_y(t_i)$ for each direction and it is discretized in a certain number of time steps $i = 0, ..., N - 1$. The two

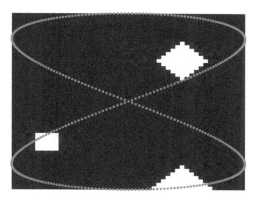

Figure 3.7: Simple phantom with basic Lissajous trajectory.

received signals for this particular phantom are shown in figure 3.8(a) The signals $u_x(t_i)$ and

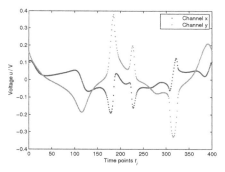

(a) Received signal for both channels $u_x(t_i)$ and $u_y(t_i)$.

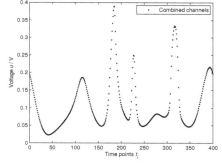

(b) Signals $u_x(t_i)$ and $u_y(t_i)$ vectorized to one signal $u_{xy}(t_i)$.

Figure 3.8: (a) Received channel signals and (b) their combined signal.

$u_y(t_i)$ are superposed with the help of

$$u_{xy}(t_i) = \sqrt{u_x(t_i)^2 + u_y(t_i)^2}. \tag{3.5.20}$$

The combined signal $u_{xy}(t_i)$ seen in figure 3.8(b) shows the three peaks caused by the three structures in the phantom. The combined signal has to be normalized by the velocity of the FFP because the magnitude of the received signal depends on the change rate of the magnetic field. The adjusted signal in figure 3.9(a) with the velocity of the FFP is presented in figure 3.9(b).

In practise, the signal $u_{xy}(t)$ is only normalized by a time depending parameter, so the equation

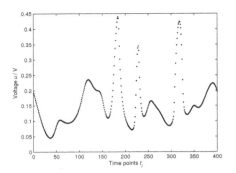
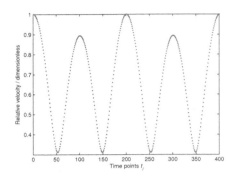

(a) Normalized signal $s_{xy}(t)$ by the velocity of the FFP.

(b) Velocity of the FFP for the basic Lissajous trajectory.

Figure 3.9: (a) Normalized signal and (b) Velocity of the FFP.

3.5.9 is simplified to

$$Img(\boldsymbol{r}(t)) = \frac{u_{xy}(t)}{||\dot{\boldsymbol{r}}_s(t)||} \qquad (3.5.21)$$

As a next step, the field of view is discretized in X times Y pixel for each dimension. Then for each pixel (x, y) the time points $(t_k, ..., t_l)$ are collected at which time point the FFP is within the pixel and in this parts of the field of view respectively. This set can be written as

$$\boldsymbol{r}_{FFP}(t_k, ..., t_l) \in \text{pixel}(x, y) = \text{field of view}(\frac{SizeX}{X}x, \frac{SizeY}{Y}y), \qquad (3.5.22)$$

where $SizeX$ and $SizeY$ are the size of the field of view in meter. The value of the pixel(x, y) is assigned with the sum

$$\text{pixel}(x, y) = \frac{1}{P} \sum_{i=k}^{l} u(t_i) \qquad (3.5.23)$$

of all signal values $u(t_i)$ at the time points $(t_k, ..., t_l)$, when the FFP is within that area. $P = l - k$ is the total number of time points within the area. This simple approach is done for every pixel (x, y) to reconstructed the whole native image. The scheme of the regridding process can be seen in figure 3.10. The reconstructed native image for the simple example with basic Lissajous trajectory and ordinary phantom is illustrated in figure 3.11. The three structures in the phantom can be identified by the brigther pixel in the image. This approach could be optimized by weighting the signal values for one pixel according to their distance to the center of the pixel.

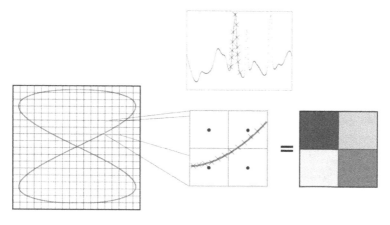

Figure 3.10: Scheme of regridding process.

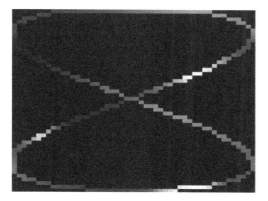

Figure 3.11: Reconstructed native image with basic Lissajous trajectory.

3.5.2 Deconvolution

The deconvolution describes the inversion of the convolution and is schematically shown in figure 3.12. The convolution formulates the process when an image is convolved with a point spread function and results in a blurred image. The deconvolution reverses this process by deconvolving, the blurred image with the PSF. It tries to restore the original image. A convolution can always be calculated but it is not always possible to perform a deconvolution since information can be lost during the convolution process. The easiest way of performing the deconvolution is the use of the convolution theorem. It states that the convolution in the time domain

$$Img = c * \dot{\mathcal{L}} \qquad (3.5.24)$$

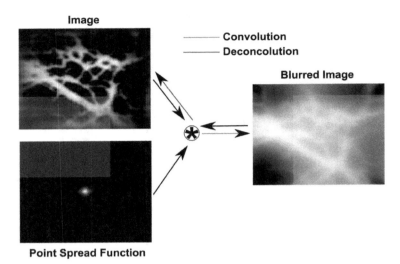

Figure 3.12: Convolution and deconvolution scheme with image, point spread function and blurred image.

is the equivalent of a multiplication in the frequency domain

$$\hat{Img} = \hat{c} \cdot \hat{\mathcal{L}}. \tag{3.5.25}$$

The deconvolution is then realized by the quotient

$$\hat{c} = \frac{\hat{Img}}{\hat{\mathcal{L}}} \tag{3.5.26}$$

in the frequency domain and the spectrum $\hat{c}$ is inverse Fourier transformed in the time domain to receive the image c.

This native approach faces several problems and that is why the deconvolution is often done by more complex algorithms such as the deconvolution with Tikhonov regularization and the Wiener deconvolution. It becomes a problem when $\hat{\mathcal{L}}$ is zero at some positions and in reality the image data is contaminated with additive noise. Both factors make the deconvolution challenging.

Deconvolution with Tikhonov regularization

The deconvolution with Tikhonov regularization basically introduces an extension parameter λ in the fraction to avoid a division by zero. The parameter λ punishes the influence of values close to zero and prevents the division by too small values, which would cause an artificially high value in the resulting image. The equation 3.5.26 is extended to the formula

$$\hat{c}(v, w) = \frac{\hat{\mathcal{L}}^*(v, w)}{\left|\hat{\mathcal{L}}(v, w)\right|^2 + \lambda^2} \hat{Img}(v, w) \tag{3.5.27}$$

and denotes the deconvolution with Tikhonov regularization, where (v, w) are the Fourier transformed coordinates to the time domain coordinates (x, y). The optimal regularization parameter λ is usually determined by plotting the square of the residuum norm

$$\left|\left|(\dot{\mathcal{L}} * c_{reg}) - Img\right|\right|_2^2 \tag{3.5.28}$$

against the square of the solution norm

$$||c_{reg}||_2^2 \tag{3.5.29}$$

logarithmically on both axes. c_{reg} describes the regularized solution of c. The parameter close to the corner of the L-curve defines the best compromise between existence and smoothness of the solution.

Wiener deconvolution

The Wiener deconvolution [38] uses the Wiener filter to minimize the noise influence in the deconvolution process. It is performed in the frequency domain and tries to reduce the impact of deconvoluted frequencies that have a low signal-to-noise ratio.

In preparation for the Wiener deconvolution an edgetaper is applied to the image. The edgetaper (edgetaper.m MATLAB©) reduces the ringing effects in deblurring methods such as the Wiener deconvolution. It blurs the edges of the already blurred image and creates an image, where the central region is equal to the original blurred image and the edges are equal to the additional blurred image. The weighted sum of the resulting image is determined by the auto-correlation function of the PSF.

In figure 3.13(b) the original blurred image is shown and in figure 3.13(a) the edgetaper was applied to the original blurred image. One can see that the edges are much more blurred than in the original image.

The Wiener deconvolution assumes that the signal $c(x, y)$ is superposed with noise $n(x, y)$.

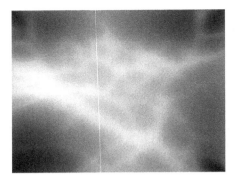 

(a) Original blurred image.   (b) Image with applied edgetaper and additional
                                               blurred edges.

Figure 3.13: (a) Original image and (b) edgetaper applied to blurred image.

The system is then described by

$$Img(x,y) = \dot{\mathcal{L}}(x,y) * (c(x,y) + n(x,y)), \tag{3.5.30}$$

where $Img(x,y)$ is the result of the convolution in the time domain. The additive noise is independent of the signal $c(x,y)$ and $\dot{\mathcal{L}}(x,y)$ denotes the point spread function of a time-invariant linear system. The Wiener deconvolution is given in the frequency domain by

$$\hat{c}(v,w) = \frac{\hat{\dot{\mathcal{L}}}^*(v,w)\hat{s}(v,w)}{\left|\hat{\dot{\mathcal{L}}}(v,w)\right|^2 \hat{s}(v,w) + \hat{n}(v,w)} \hat{Img}(v,w) \tag{3.5.31}$$

where $\hat{s}(v,w) = \mathbb{E}\left|\hat{c}(v,w)\right|^2$ denotes the mean spectral power density of the signal $c(x,y)$ and $\hat{n}(v,w) = \mathbb{E}\left|\hat{n}(v,w)\right|^2$ describes the mean spectral power density of the noise $n(x,y)$. The Fourier transformed PSF is given by $\hat{\dot{\mathcal{L}}}(v,w)$ and the Fourier transformation of the received signal $Img(x,y)$ is written as $\hat{Img}(v,w)$.

The filter operation can be rearranged to

$$\frac{\hat{\dot{\mathcal{L}}}^*(v,w)\hat{s}(v,w)}{\left|\hat{\dot{\mathcal{L}}}(v,w)\right|^2 \hat{s}(v,w) + \hat{n}(v,w)} = \frac{1}{\hat{\dot{\mathcal{L}}}(v,w)} \left[\frac{\left|\hat{\dot{\mathcal{L}}}(v,w)\right|^2}{\left|\hat{\dot{\mathcal{L}}}(v,w)\right|^2 + \frac{\hat{n}(v,w)}{\hat{s}(v,w)}} \right] \tag{3.5.32}$$

$$= \frac{1}{\hat{\dot{\mathcal{L}}}(v,w)} \left[\frac{\left|\hat{\dot{\mathcal{L}}}(v,w)\right|^2}{\left|\hat{\dot{\mathcal{L}}}(v,w)\right|^2 + \frac{1}{SNR(v,w)}} \right]. \tag{3.5.33}$$

When the signal-to-noise ratio $SNR(v,w) = \hat{s}(v,w)/\hat{n}(v,w)$ becomes infinity, meaning that there is no noise, the fraction in the square brackets will become one and the deconvolution will be the same as in equation 3.5.26. The Wiener filter attenuates frequencies dependent on their signal-to-noise ratio. That means if the noise increases at a frequency, the SNR drops and the term in the square brackets becomes smaller. In this work the $NSR = 1/SNR$ is varied with the parameter τ to ensure a moderate Wiener deconvolution. Therefore, the artifacts are minimized and it can be identified when the image is over-deconvolved.

3.6 Advantages and disadvantages of frequency and x-space reconstruction

This section fulfils the purpose of summarizing the key characteristics of frequency and x-space reconstruction. Neither technique has proven to be superior to the other so far. Each technique comes with limitations and drawbacks while relying on different prerequisites.

The frequency reconstruction with its system matrix probably provides the more exact reconstruction as it withholds the individual characteristics of the scanner and the particles. But the system matrix has the drawback that its acquisition time is far too long especially for 3D. Attempts to reduce the acquisition time by using a model-based system matrix have not been as satisfactory as wished [12]. The non-perfect coil geometry and the anisotropy appear to be the problem in the modeling process. Further challenges occur though the noise introduced in measured system matrix, the memory demand of the system matrix, and the runtime intensive solving of a huge linear equation system.

The x-space reconstruction, however, does not need the system matrix and provides a simple and easy to handle reconstruction technique. But all these advantages do not come along for free. The gradient field needs to be very homogeneous in order to ensure the characteristics of a linear, space invariant (LSI) imaging technique. A very homogeneous excitation field need to be given with a high gradient and a small field of view. Therefore, Goodwill et al. scanned many small fields of view and moved the field of view sequently around the desired size of a huge field of view. The reconstructed images of the small fields of view were stitched together to one combined image later [15]. This inconvenient procedure takes a lot of time and cause the x-space reconstruction to lose its real-time ability. The real-time ability underlines one key advantage of the frequency reconstruction. However, x-space reconstruction yields to non real-time applications.

In the next chapter the simulation results between both techniques are compared for different parameters. For an objective comparison the root mean square deviation is used.

Normalized root mean square deviation

The normalized root mean square deviation (NRMSD) is used to analyse the performance of the reconstruction. It provides an objective evaluation between the different deconvolution methods and different reconstruction techniques. The error value

$$E_{NRMSD} = \frac{\sqrt{\sum_{i=1}^{N} \sum_{j=1}^{M} (P_{i,j} - c_{i,j})/(N \cdot M)}}{\max(P, c) - \min(P, c)} \qquad (3.6.1)$$

is calculated with the help of the belonging phantom $P_{i,j}$ and the resulted image $c_{i,j}$. The NRMSD is a good measurement of the differences between the values predicted by a model and the actually observed values [39].

4 Results

In this chapter, the x-space reconstruction is shown for four different phantoms using the ideal scanner with a homogeneous magnetic field. The resulting native images are presented and the shape of the PSF is analysed. With the help of the PSF two different deconvolution techniques namely the Wiener deconvolution and the regularization with Tikhonov are compared. The normalized root mean square error is calculated for both deconvolution techniques in order to compare them objectively.

In the next section, deconvolved x-space images are compared to the frequency reconstructed images. To achieve a wider understanding, several parameter combination are used for the comparison. The sampling rate and the density of the Lissajous trajectory are mainly adjusted to find detailed differences when which method yields the best results.

Thirdly, the x-space reconstruction is simulated on a realistic MPI scanner with a classical coil setup and with an almost homogeneous magnetic field. Here, the strength of the gradient field is varied.

4.1 X-space reconstruction with an ideal scanner in 2D

The x-space reconstruction in 2D was done by regarding several parameters. The choice of these parameters determines the quality of the reconstructed images. The parameters have been chosen to be quite realistic so that it would also be possible to transform this settings into practise.

Hence, the parameters that have the most important influence on the reconstruction process are listed here:

- Gradient

- Field of view

- Shape of the reconstructed image

- Density of the Lissajous trajectory

- Sampling rate

- Nanoparticle diameter.

The **gradient** is set to $[G_x, G_y, G_z] = [-0.5, -0.5, 1]$ T/m, which is relative low gradient. The gradient by Gleich et al. [1] has been set to $[G_x, G_y, G_z] = [3.4, -1.7, -1.7]$ T/m and Goodwill et al. [40] used a gradient of $[G_x, G_y, G_z] = [6, -3, -3]$ T/m. Note that adjusting the gradient will affect the resolution inverse proportionally.

The **field of view** is set to $[Size_x, Size_y, Size_z] = [0.05, 0.05, 0.0001]$ m and corresponds to the desired size of the field of view.
The classical MPI scanner has a field of view of $[Size_x, Size_y, Size_z] = [0.016, 0.016, 0.0001]$ m, which can be used for mice experiments.

The **shape** of the reconstructed image determines with how many pixels the image is discretized. The more pixels are used the smoother the image appeals. With the field of view and the shape it is also possible to identify how much distance in meter one pixel represents. Here, the shape is set to $[Shape_x, Shape_y, Shape_z] = [100, 100, 1]$ pixel which means that one pixel for example represents 0.5 mm for the FOV $[Size_x, Size_y, Size_z] = [0.05, 0.05, 0.0001]$ m.

The **density** of the Lissajous trajectory determines how dense the trajectory has sampled the field of view. The parameter of $N = 32$ corresponds to excitation frequencies $[f_x, f_y] = [26041, 26881]$ Hz and means that the real-time condition for 3D is still matched.
The parameter of $N = 100$ corresponds to excitation frequencies $[f_x, f_y] = [25000, 25253]$ Hz and amounts that the real-time condition for 3D is not matched but only the 2D condition.

The **sampling rate** determines how many discrete values are taken during the path of the trajectory. With the help of the time for one period of the trajectory the number of points is calculated. The sampling rate is set to $f_{samp} = 10^7$ Hz and that results in 12000 time points when the trajectory repetition time is 0.0012 s.

The **nanoparticle diameter** is set to $d = 50$ nm and is essential for the resolution as mentioned before.

In this simulation study four different phantoms seen in figure 4.1 are used to analyse the quality and resolution of the x-space method. The **resolution phantom** consists of four different areas with circles in it that have a different diameter in each area. The diameters of the circles are $[2, 3, 4, 5]$ mm and the phantom can be seen in figure 4.1(a).
The **IMT logo phantom** represents sharp straight lines and determines whether the x-space

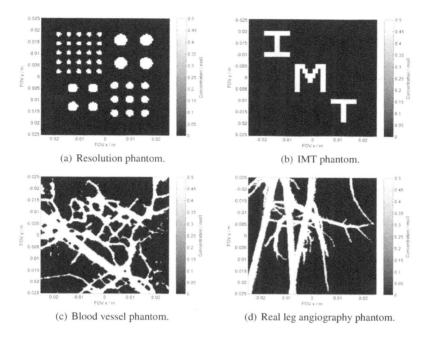

(a) Resolution phantom.

(b) IMT phantom.

(c) Blood vessel phantom.

(d) Real leg angiography phantom.

Figure 4.1: Four different phantoms, (a) the resolution phantom determines to what extent the reconstruction resolves the circles with different diameters, (b) the IMT phantom serves a show-off purpose, (c) and (d) helps to visualize what the application of MPI could look like.

method can reconstruct these lines without blurring. It is depicted in figure 4.1(b).

The **blood vessel phantom** [41] shown in figure 4.1(c) and the **leg angiography phantom** [42] presented in figure 4.1(d) are supposed to show the idea of future applications. It remains the question if it is possible to resolve the very fine blood vessel and their bifurcation.

The point spread function is determined by setting the nanoparticle concentration to one pixel in the middle of the field of view and then the native image is reconstructed.

The PSF as a 2D image can be seen in figure 4.2(a) and the 3D surf plot with colormap hot is depicted in figure 4.2(b). The colormap hot was chosen to achieve a better visual contrast of the PSF.

Since the magnetic field of the ideal scanner is homogeneous, the PSF is equal at every position of the field of view.

The native reconstructed images of the four phantoms are shown in figure 4.3. The native image of the resolution phantom clearly resolves all circles in the four areas. Even the smallest circles are visible. The native image resembles the phantom quite well but is appears more blurred.

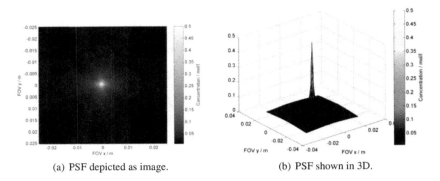

(a) PSF depicted as image.   (b) PSF shown in 3D.

Figure 4.2: The PSF is shown as a 2D image in (a) and has been depicted as a 3D surf plot (b) with colormap hot to achieve a better visual contrast.

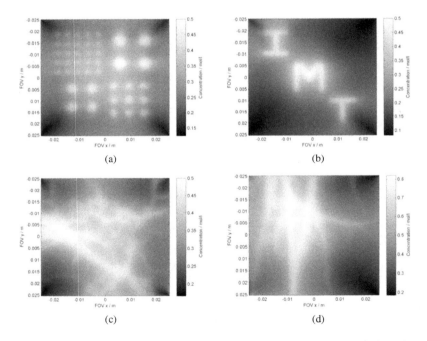

(a)   (b)

(c)   (d)

Figure 4.3: The native reconstructed images of the four phantoms, (a) resolution phantom reconstruction, (b) IMT logo reconstruction, (c) blood vessel reconstruction, (d) leg angiography reconstruction.

The blurring was expected and will be dealt with in the deconvolution step. The reconstruced resolution phantom is shown in figure 4.10(d).

The native image reconstructed the IMT phantom easily and it is also blurred as expected at the edges of the font. It is presented in figure 4.3(b).

The blood vessel structure of both blood vessel and leg angiography phantom have been reconstructed satisfactorily in the native image. Although the very fine blood vessel fade in the blurring of the bigger ones, they can be identified at all. The native image of the blood vessel phantom is depicted in figure 4.3(c), while the native image of the leg angiography phantom is shown in figure 4.3(d).

As a next step, the deconvolution process is performed by using two different deconvolution techniques. The deconvolution with Tikhonov regularization and the Wiener deconvolution are compared for various regularization parameter λ_i and τ_i shown in figure 4.4, 4.5, 4.6, and 4.7. The value of the regularization parameter $\lambda_1 < \lambda_2 < \lambda_3 < \lambda_4 < \lambda_5$ increases with its index and the influence of the regularization grows. It means that the images become smoother with increasing λ_i.

The results for the deconvolution with Tikhonov regularization depending on the different λ_i are shown in figure 4.4, 4.5, 4.6, and 4.7. It can be seen that the first Tikhonov reconstruction with λ_1 is affected by noise and the following images with $\lambda_2 - \lambda_5$ are much smoother. The blurring is still there but has become less visual.

The results of the Wiener deconvolution are shown in figure 4.4, 4.5, 4.6, and 4.7. The first results of the Wiener deconvolution with τ_1 is also affected by noise and additionally linear artifacts are added horizontally and vertically by the deconvolution process. In the following images with $\tau_2 - \tau_5$ the noise disappears but the linear artifacts remain although they are becoming less visible. The Wiener deconvolution completely deblurres the native images but some very fine blood vessel structures are not resolved any more.

The normalized root mean square error for the Tikhonov and the Wiener deconvolution with different parameters λ_i and τ_i for the four phantoms is shown in figure 4.8(a), 4.8(b), 4.8(c), and 4.8(d). It becomes evident that the error of the Tikhonov deconvolution stays between $0.45 - 0.58$ for the resolution phantom, $0.3 - 0.4$ for the IMT phantom, $0.5 - 0.55$ for the blood vessel phantom, and $0.5 - 0.55$ for the leg angiography phantom, while it does not improve for higher values of λ. The error of the Wiener deconvolution is between $0.2 - 0.25$ for the resolution phantom, $0.17 - 0.2$ for the IMT phantom, $0.35 - 0.38$ for the blood vessel phantom, and $0.32 - 0.38$ for the leg angiography phantom, and it does improve slightly but raises again when the parameter value τ becomes too high.

The optimal regularization parameter can either be found by visual evaluation or with the help of the L-curve plot. As mentioned before, the square of the residual norm and the square of the result norm are plotted logarithmically on both axes. The corner of the L-curve plot usually defines the best balance between deconvolution and regularization. The L-curve of the Tikhonov regularization of the resolution phantom is exemplarily shown in figure 4.9 for the five deconvolved images with $\lambda_1 - \lambda_5$.

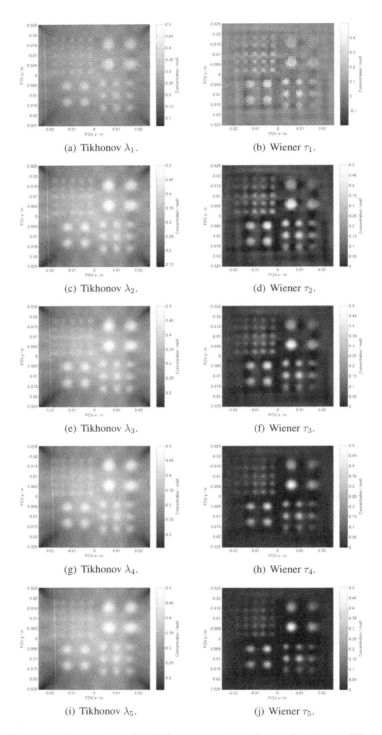

(a) Tikhonov λ_1.   (b) Wiener τ_1.

(c) Tikhonov λ_2.   (d) Wiener τ_2.

(e) Tikhonov λ_3.   (f) Wiener τ_3.

(g) Tikhonov λ_4.   (h) Wiener τ_4.

(i) Tikhonov λ_5.   (j) Wiener τ_5.

Figure 4.4: Deconvolution results with Tikhonov regularization (left column), Wiener deconvolution (rigth column) for the resolution phantom.

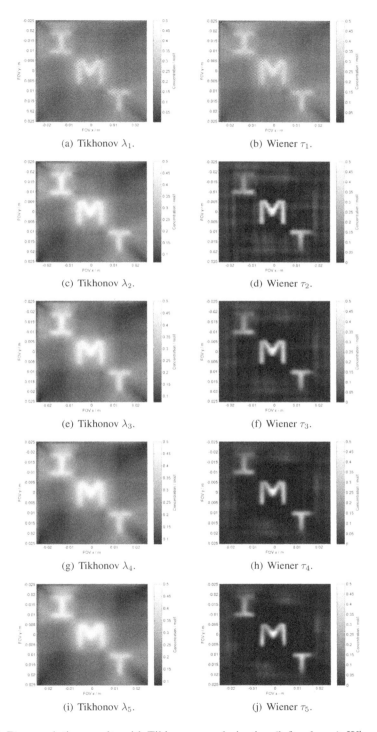

(a) Tikhonov λ_1.

(b) Wiener τ_1.

(c) Tikhonov λ_2.

(d) Wiener τ_2.

(e) Tikhonov λ_3.

(f) Wiener τ_3.

(g) Tikhonov λ_4.

(h) Wiener τ_4.

(i) Tikhonov λ_5.

(j) Wiener τ_5.

Figure 4.5: Deconvolution results with Tikhonov regularization (left column), Wiener deconvolution (rigth column) for the IMT phantom.

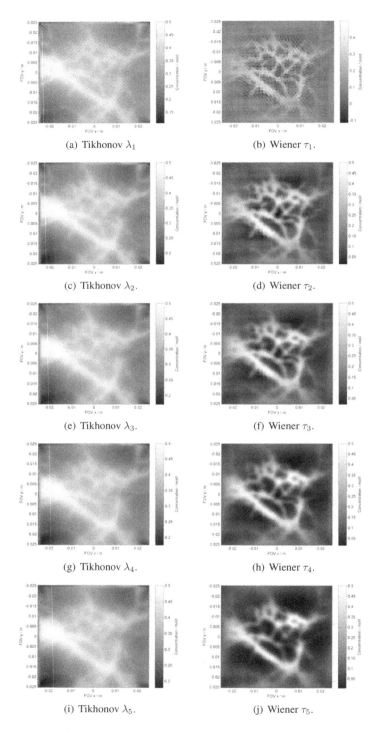

(a) Tikhonov λ_1 (b) Wiener τ_1.

(c) Tikhonov λ_2.   (d) Wiener τ_2.

(e) Tikhonov λ_3.   (f) Wiener τ_3.

(g) Tikhonov λ_4.   (h) Wiener τ_4.

(i) Tikhonov λ_5.   (j) Wiener τ_5.

Figure 4.6: Deconvolution results with Tikhonov regularization (left column), Wiener deconvolution (rigth column) for the blood vessel phantom.

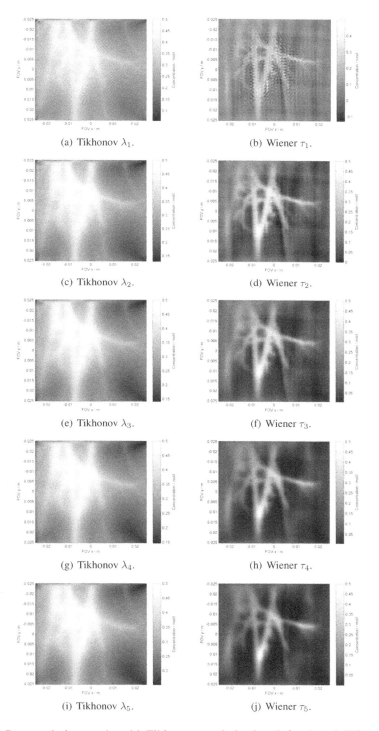

(a) Tikhonov λ_1.   (b) Wiener τ_1.

(c) Tikhonov λ_2.   (d) Wiener τ_2.

(e) Tikhonov λ_3.   (f) Wiener τ_3.

(g) Tikhonov λ_4.   (h) Wiener τ_4.

(i) Tikhonov λ_5.   (j) Wiener τ_5.

Figure 4.7: Deconvolution results with Tikhonov regularization (left column), Wiener deconvolution (rigth column) for the leg angiography phantom.

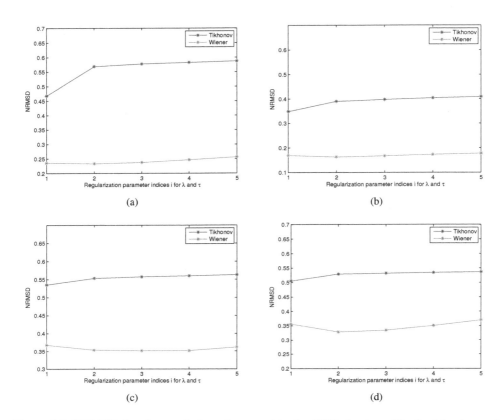

Figure 4.8: NRMSD for the resolution phantom (a), the IMT phantom (b), the blood vessel phantom (c), and the leg angiography phantom (d) with Tikhonov deconvolution with λ_i and τ_i for the Wiener deconvolution.

The optimal deconvolved images of the phantoms are chosen regarding the visual perception, the L-curve and the NRMSD. The result of the deconvolution with Tikhonov regularization in figure 4.4(c) still shows signs of noise but otherwise the smallest circles would be smoothed too much and would not be visible any more.

The Wiener deconvolution in figure 4.4(f) works quite well on the resolution phantom. The linear artifacts are barely recognizable and the blurring is completely vanished. The corners of the image appear darker which is probably caused by the edgetaper.

The result for the IMT phantom shows a very good result for the Wiener deconvolution in figure 4.5(d) and has the lowest NRMSD. With the Tikhonov regularization the deconvolved image 4.5(c) is still satisfying, but the image appeals still blurred.

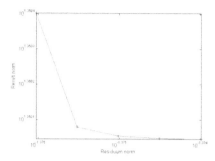

Figure 4.9: L-curve of the Tikhonov regularization.

The resulting images of the Wiener deconvolution applied to the blood vessel and leg angiography phantom are shown in figure 4.6(d), and 4.7(d). The Wiener deconvolution for the blood vessels provides good results. The blurring has been removed and the blood vessel structure is clearly visible although some very fine structures got lost close to the corners.

The results of the Tikhonov regularized blood vessel phantoms in figure 4.6(c), and 4.7(c) are similar to each other. The blurring is not entirely vanished and little noise is added to the image although the very fine blood vessels can be still identified.

X-space reconstruction with different trajectory density and sampling rate

In the following simulation study, the influence of the density of the Lissajous trajectory and the sampling rate is evaluated. The parameter N for the density of the Lissajous trajectory is set to $N = 32$ and $N = 100$ with frequencies $[f_x, f_y] = [26041, 26881]$ Hz and $[f_x, f_y] = [25000, 25253]$ Hz. The sampling rate is varied between $f_{samp} = 10^6$ Hz, $f_{samp} = 10^7$ Hz, and $f_{samp} = 10^8$ Hz. The native image results of these simulations are shown in figure 4.10.

In figure 4.10(a) the reconstruction did not come to a satisfactory result, because the density of the Lissajous trajectory and the sampling rate were chosen too low and not enough information could be assigned to all pixel. The resulting image shown in figure 4.10(b) shows that all pixels were allocated with enough information but the image is extremely blurred which indicates that the sampling rate was not high enough. If only the sampling rate is increased to $f_{samp} = 10^7$ Hz as in figure 4.10(c), the distribution of the circles of the resolution phantom can be identified but the whole image appears quite noisy due to the fact that some pixel remain unsigned. The image in figure 4.10(d), where the sampling rate and the density were increased, shows a promising result since all circles of the resolution phantom are clearly visible, even the smallest ones, and every pixel has been allocated with information. If the density of the Lissajous trajectory is kept by $N = 32$ and the sampling rate is increased to $f_{samp} = 10^8$ Hz, the resulting image seen in

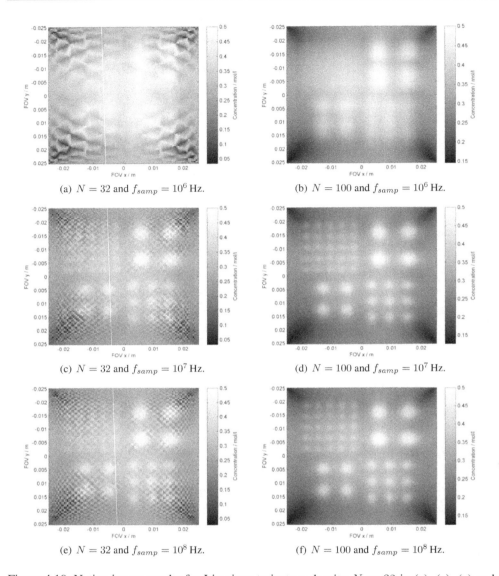

Figure 4.10: Native image results for Lissajous trajectory density $N = 32$ in (a), (c), (e) and $N = 100$ in (b), (d), (f). The sampling rate is increased with each row from 10^6 Hz to 10^8 Hz.

figure 4.10(e) suffers from the same problems as the result in figure 4.10(c). By increasing the density of the Lissajous trajectory to $N = 100$ and the sampling rate to $f_{samp} = 10^8$ Hz, the image quality 4.10(f) is still improved compared to image 4.10(d) but the improvement is not magnificently high.

4.2 Comparison between x-space and frequency reconstruction with an ideal scanner in 2D

In this section the results of the x-space algorithm deconvolved with Wiener deconvolution are compared with the frequency space reconstructed images. The x-space deconvolved images are shown for the different parameter combinations of density and sampling rate.

Nevertheless, the native results 4.10(c), and 4.10(e) are shown in figure 4.13(a), and 4.15(a) because the deconvolution failed due to the noisy appearance of the image and the less dense trajectory.

The results of the frequency reconstruction are only shown for the parameter combination $N = 32$ and $f_{samp} = 10^6$ Hz since the simulation tool failed to reconstruct the images for higher parameter combination due to memory allocation problems caused by the huge system matrix.

For the parameter combination $N = 32$ and $f_{samp} = 10^6$ Hz the frequency reconstruction im-

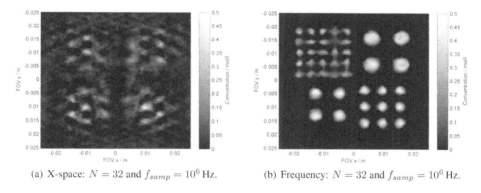

(a) X-space: $N = 32$ and $f_{samp} = 10^6$ Hz.　　　(b) Frequency: $N = 32$ and $f_{samp} = 10^6$ Hz.

Figure 4.11: X-space reconstruction (a) and frequency reconstruction (b) for Lissajous trajectory density $N = 32$ and sampling rate 10^6 Hz.

age seen in figure 4.11(b) is used as a reference for the following comparisons. It clearly shows a higher image quality of the reconstruction phantom. Only the circles in the upper left corner of the resolution phantom are not completely resolved, where as in the x-space reconstructed image 4.11(a) non of the circles could be resolved. If the density of the Lissajous trajectory is increased with $N = 100$ for the x-space reconstruction, the frequency reconstruction seen in figure 4.12(b) still resolves the phantom very well while the x-space reconstruction seen in figure 4.12(a) is only able to distinguish between the circles in the upper right corner and in the lower left corner.

If the sampling rate is raised to $f_{samp} = 10^7$ Hz and the density of the trajectory is kept to the repetition time of the 3D condition with $N = 32$, the x-space reconstructed image in figure

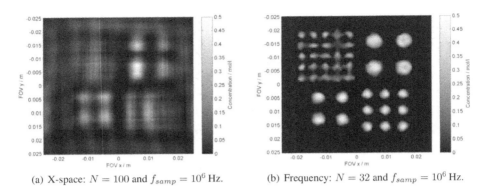

(a) X-space: $N = 100$ and $f_{samp} = 10^6$ Hz.   (b) Frequency: $N = 32$ and $f_{samp} = 10^6$ Hz.

Figure 4.12: Deconvolved x-space result for Lissajous trajectory density $N = 100$ and $f_{samp} = 10^6$ Hz in (a) and frequency reconstruction with $N = 32$ and sampling rate 10^6 Hz in (b).

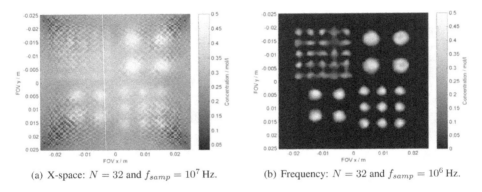

(a) X-space: $N = 32$ and $f_{samp} = 10^7$ Hz.   (b) Frequency: $N = 32$ and $f_{samp} = 10^6$ Hz.

Figure 4.13: X-space native image for Lissajous trajectory density $N = 32$ and $f_{samp} = 10^6$ Hz in (a) and frequency reconstruction with $N = 32$ and sampling rate 10^6 Hz in (b).

4.13(a), here as a native image, is able to resolve all circles of the resolution phantom except the smallest ones and the image still appears quite blurry and noisy.

By increasing both the sampling rate to $f_{samp} = 10^7$ Hz and the density to $N = 100$, the x-space reconstructed image seen in figure 4.18(a) looks very satisfying. All circle sizes of the resolution phantom are resolved.

With a density determined by the parameter $N = 32$ and a sampling rate of $f_{samp} = 10^8$ Hz, the x-space reconstructed image seen in figure 4.15(a) can resolve the circles quite satisfying but still suffers from blurring and noise.

If the sampling rate and the density are raised to $f_{samp} = 10^8$ Hz and $N = 100$, the x-space image seen in figure 4.16(a) is only slightly improved and the frequency reconstructed image in figure 4.16(b) has a similar image quality.

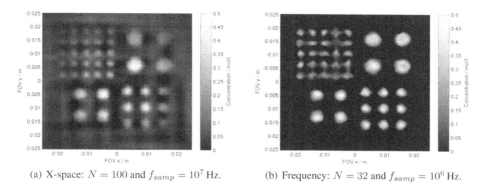

(a) X-space: $N = 100$ and $f_{samp} = 10^7$ Hz. (b) Frequency: $N = 32$ and $f_{samp} = 10^6$ Hz.

Figure 4.14: Deconvolved x-space reconstructed image for Lissajous trajectory density $N = 100$ and $f_{samp} = 10^7$ Hz in (a) and frequency reconstruction with $N = 32$ and $f_{samp} = 10^6$ Hz in (b).

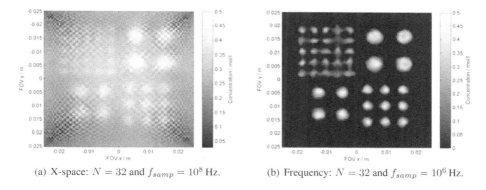

(a) X-space: $N = 32$ and $f_{samp} = 10^8$ Hz. (b) Frequency: $N = 32$ and $f_{samp} = 10^6$ Hz.

Figure 4.15: X-space native image for Lissajous trajectory density $N = 32$ and $f_{samp} = 10^8$ Hz in (a) and $N = 100$ and frequency reconstruction with $N = 32$ and $f_{samp} = 10^6$ Hz in (b).

In figure 4.17(a) the normalized root mean square deviation has been depicted with all parameter combinations p1 ($N = 32$, $f_{samp} = 10^6$ Hz), p2 ($N = 100$, $f_{samp} = 10^6$ Hz), p3 ($N = 32$, $f_{samp} = 10^7$ Hz), p4 ($N = 100$, $f_{samp} = 10^7$ Hz), p5 ($N = 32$, $f_{samp} = 10^8$ Hz), and p6 ($N = 100$, $f_{samp} = 10^7$ Hz) for the previously presented images of both reconstruction methods. What had already become evident through the visual comparison, is verified through comparison of the NRMSD values. The x-space NRMSD values decreasing with increasing parameter combination until parameter combination p4 is reached. The NRMSD of the frequency reconstruction is in general lower as the error of the reconstructed x-space images, although the parameter combination is not increased.

In figure 4.18(a) the x-space reconstructed image of the IMT phantom is shown for the parameter combination p4, which had the lowest x-space NRMSD seen in figure 4.17(b). The

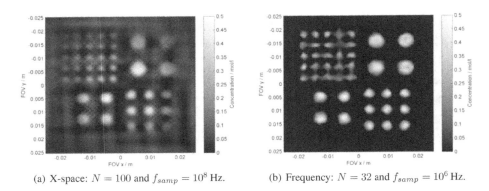

(a) X-space: $N = 100$ and $f_{samp} = 10^8$ Hz.   (b) Frequency: $N = 32$ and $f_{samp} = 10^6$ Hz.

Figure 4.16: Deconvolved x-space image with $N = 100$ and $f_{samp} = 10^8$ Hz in (a) and frequency reconstruction with $N = 32$ and $f_{samp} = 10^6$ Hz in (b).

frequency recnstruction of the IMT phantom is presented for the parameter combination p1 in figure 4.18(b) and showed an even lower NRMSD 4.17(b) as the x-space reconstructed image.

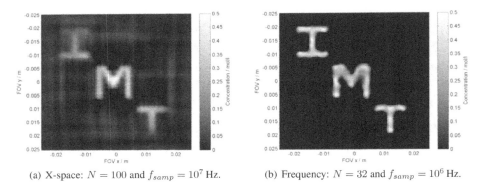

(a) X-space: $N = 100$ and $f_{samp} = 10^7$ Hz.   (b) Frequency: $N = 32$ and $f_{samp} = 10^6$ Hz.

Figure 4.18: Deconvolved x-space image with $N = 100$ and $f_{samp} = 10^7$ Hz in (a) and frequency reconstruction with $N = 32$ and $f_{samp} = 10^6$ Hz in (b).

The deconvolved x-space image of the blood vessel phantom is depicted for the parameter combination p4 in figure 4.19(a) and its lowest NRMSD is given in figure 4.17(b). The frequency reconstruction of the blood vessel phantom has a lower NRMSD also seen in figure 4.17(b). Its visual result for the parameter combination p1 can be seen in figure 4.19(b).

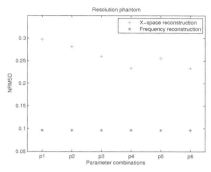 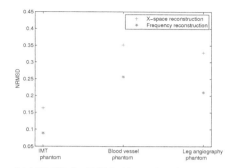

(a) NRMSD for resolution phantom.

(b) NRMSD for IMT, bold vessel and leg angiography phantom.

Figure 4.17: NRMSD for all parameter combination p1 ($N = 32$, $f_{samp} = 10^6$ Hz), p2 ($N = 100$, $f_{samp} = 10^6$ Hz), p3 ($N = 32$, $f_{samp} = 10^7$ Hz), p4 ($N = 100$, $f_{samp} = 10^7$ Hz), p5 ($N = 32$, $f_{samp} = 10^8$ Hz), and p6 ($N = 100$, $f_{samp} = 10^7$ Hz) of the resolution phantom comparing both reconstruction techniques in (a), NRMSD for parameter combination p4 for the IMT, blood vessel and leg angiography phantom in (b).

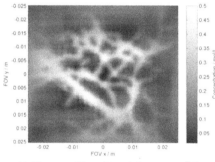 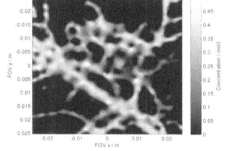

(a) X-space: $N = 100$ and $f_{samp} = 10^7$ Hz.

(b) Frequency: $N = 32$ and $f_{samp} = 10^6$ Hz.

Figure 4.19: Deconvolved x-space image with $N = 100$ and $f_{samp} = 10^7$ Hz in (a) and frequency reconstruction with $N = 32$ and $f_{samp} = 10^6$ Hz in (b).

For the parameter combination p4 the x-space reconstructed image of the leg angiography phantom is illustrated in figure 4.20(a). Its NRMSD is shown in figure 4.17(a) toegther with the NRMSD of the frequency reconstruction of the leg angiography phantom. Again, the NSMSD of the frequency reconstruction is lower as of the x-space reconstruction, which can also be seen in figure 4.20(b) when comparing it to figure 4.20(a).

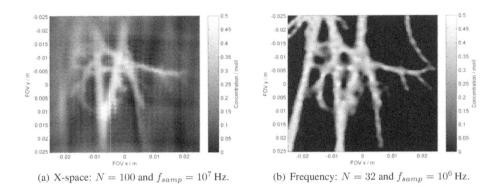

(a) X-space: $N = 100$ and $f_{samp} = 10^7$ Hz.   (b) Frequency: $N = 32$ and $f_{samp} = 10^6$ Hz.

Figure 4.20: Deconvolved x-space image with $N = 100$ and $f_{samp} = 10^7$ Hz in (a) and frequency reconstruction with $N = 32$ and $f_{samp} = 10^6$ Hz in (b).

4.3 Comparison between x-space and frequency reconstruction for the classical coil geometry

In this section the frequency reconstruction and the x-space reconstruction are compared in terms of a different gradient G_{DC} using the MPI scanner with classical coil design. For the

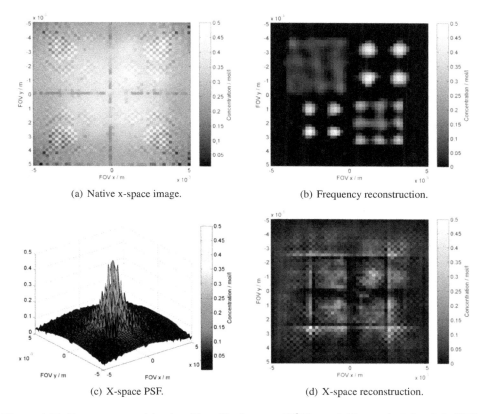

(a) Native x-space image.

(b) Frequency reconstruction.

(c) X-space PSF.

(d) X-space reconstruction.

Figure 4.21: Parameter combination $N = 32$, $f_{samp} = 10^6$ Hz, and $G_{DC} = [-0.5 \ -0.5 \ 1]$ T/m: (a) native x-space image, (b) frequency reconstruction, (c) PSF, and (d) x-space reconstruction.

MPI scanner with classical coil design different parameters are assumed. The field of view is only $[0.01, \ 0.01, \ 0.0001]$ m and the shape is changed to $[50, \ 50, \ 1]$ pixel. The gradient is varied between $G_{DC} = [-0.5, \ -0.5, \ 1]$ T/m, $G_{DC} = [-2.5, \ -2.5, \ 5]$ T/m, and $G_{DC} = [-5.5, \ -5.5, \ 11]$ T/m. The rest of the parameters is kept to the previous values. The circles in the resolution phantom have a different diameter accordingly and their values are $[0.4, \ 1, \ 0.8, \ 0.6]$ mm. For the deconvolution of the x-space images only the Wiener deconvolution has been used.

The reconstructed results for the parameter combination $G_{DC} = [-0.5, \ -0.5, \ 1]\,\text{T/m}$, $N = 32$, and $f_{samp} = 10^6\,\text{Hz}$ can be seen in figure 4.21 for the resolution phantom. The frequency reconstructed image in figure 4.21(b) resolves the circles very good only the smallest ones are not distinguishable. The x-space reconstructed image is shown in figure 4.21(d) with its native image in 4.21(a) and its PSF in 4.21(c). In the x-space image the circles are not resolved at all and the PSF has a lot of small peaks. The NRMSD of both reconstructed images is given in figure 4.23(a) and underlines that the frequency reconstruction has a lower error value by about 8%.

The reconstructed results for the parameter combination $N = 32$, $f_{samp} = 10^6\,\text{Hz}$, and $G_{DC} =$

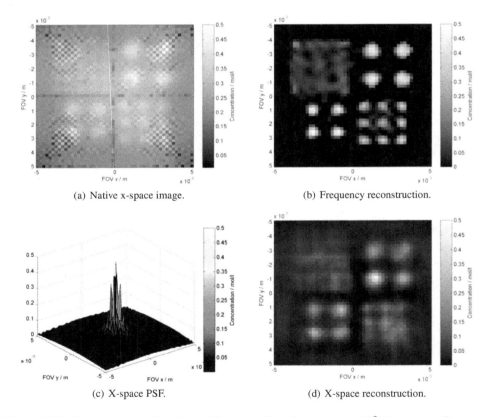

(a) Native x-space image.

(b) Frequency reconstruction.

(c) X-space PSF.

(d) X-space reconstruction.

Figure 4.22: Parameter combination $N = 32$, $f_{samp} = 10^6\,\text{Hz}$, and $G_{DC} = [-2.5, \ -2.5, \ 5]\,\text{T/m}$: (a) native x-space image, (b) frequency reconstruction, (c) PSF, and (d) x-space reconstruction.

$[-2.5, \ -2.5, \ 5]\,\text{T/m}$ are shown in figure 4.22. The x-space reconstructed image is depicted in figure 4.22(d) with its native image in figure 4.22(a) and its PSF in figure 4.22(c). The x-space image is able to resolve the bigger circles in the upper right und lower left corner while failing in resolving the smaller circles. The frequency reconstructed image in figure 4.22(b) shows only a slight improvement with a higher gradient but it can still resolve all circles except the smallest ones. Note that the PSF is tighter with the higher gradient. The NRMSD for both techniques is visible in figure 4.23(a) and it becomes again evident that the frequency reconstruction has a lower error of about 8% while the error in general is 4% lower compared to the smaller gradient.

The reconstructed results for the parameter combination $N = 32$, $f_{samp} = 10^6$ Hz, and

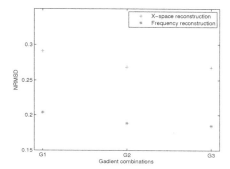

(a) NRMSD for different gradient combinations.

Figure 4.23: (a) NRMSD for the gradient combination G1 ($\boldsymbol{G}_{DC} = [-0.5, \ -0.5, \ 1]$ T/m), G2 ($\boldsymbol{G}_{DC} = [-2.5, \ -2.5, \ 5]$ T/m), and G3 ($\boldsymbol{G}_{DC} = [-5.5, \ -5.5, \ 11]$ T/m) with $N = 32$, $f_{samp} = 10^6$ Hz of the resolution phantom and both reconstruction techniques using the classical coil setup.

$\boldsymbol{G}_{DC} = [-5.5, \ -5.5, \ 11]$ T/m are presented in figure 4.24. The frequency reconstructed image in figure 4.24(b) show a very good result but the visual perception and the NRMSD seen in figure 4.23(a) have not been improved magnificently by the higher gradient. The x-space reconstructed image is seen in figure 4.24(d) with its native image in figure 4.24(a) and its PSF in figure 4.24(c). The PSF has become a little bit tighter, but the deconvolved x-space image resolves the resolution phantom only slightly better as with the previous lower gradient $\boldsymbol{G}_{DC} = [-2.5, \ -2.5, \ 5]$ T/m. The same is confirmed by the NRMSD seen in figure 4.23(a) where the error of the x-space image is at about 18% and about 8% lower as the error of the frequency reconstructed image.

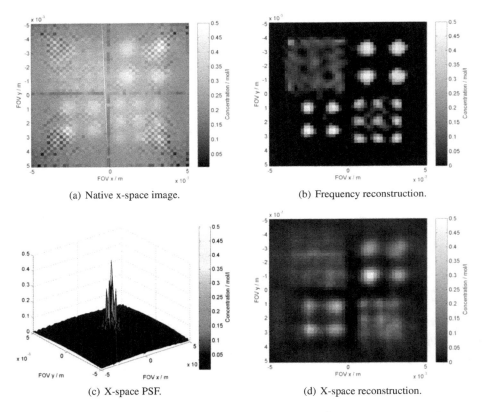

(a) Native x-space image.   (b) Frequency reconstruction.

(c) X-space PSF.   (d) X-space reconstruction.

Figure 4.24: Parameter combination $N = 32$, $f_{samp} = 10^6$ Hz, and $\boldsymbol{G}_{DC} = [-5.5\ -$
5.5 11] T/m: (a) native x-space image, (b) frequency reconstruction, (c) PSF, and
(d) x-space reconstruction.

5 Discussion

The discussion of the results is divided into three parts.

At first, the comparison between the both deconvolution techniques has been performed. The results clearly show that the Wiener deconvolution yielded better images in terms of visual perception and NRMSD. However, smaller structures such as the blood vessels located in the corner were lost during Wiener deconvolution process. This is probably due to the used edgetaper, which was applied to reduce ringing artifacts in the deconvolution. The Tikhonov deconvolution did not completely deblur the image and smoothed the edges of the objects only minimal. The visual perception of the Tikhonov reconstructed images was only slightly different from the native images. The Wiener deconvolution has also been used by Goodwill et al., but it requires further research whether the Wiener deconvolution remains the best deconvolution technique for x-space MPI.

Secondly, the frequency reconstruction and the x-space reconstruction with Lissajous trajectory were compared on an ideal scanner regarding different trajectory densities and sampling rates. The results clearly showed that the frequency reconstruction performed better in terms of resolution and image quality. The x-space reconstruction needed a denser trajectory and a higher sampling rate in order to achieve results that are almost equal to the frequency reconstructed images. Of course, the x-space reconstruction does not require the system function and the achieved images are instantly available, but by increasing the density and the sampling rate the x-space reconstruction would lose its real-time ability. That could be solved by increasing the excitation frequency from about 25 kHz to 125 kHz. Then the repetition time of the trajectory would be smaller and a denser trajectory could be used that still matches the 3D real-time condition. As an alternative, the phase shift of the excitation frequency could be used to test the performance of x-space with a denser trajectory without modifying the hardware too much.

Thirdly, the x-space reconstruction and the frequency reconstruction were compared on an MPI scanner with classical coil design regrading different gradients. The results clearly showed that the frequency reconstruction achieved superior results when comparing the visual perception and the NRMSD. The x-space reconstruction performed only satisfying with high gradients.

Since the FOV is relatively small, it is possible to generate a homogeneous magnetic field with a high gradient, but when the FOV increases it becomes challenging to keep the homogeneity of the magnetic field for a high gradient. However, the frequency reconstruction also faces challenges when the FOV is increased. The acquiring time of the system function will become enormous and a huge calculation effort has to be made to invert the system matrix. An attempt to reduced the acquisition time has been made by [43], and [44], which achieved a great reduction by using a hybrid system function. Further research will show whether the system function can be modeled by a more precise physical model. That would make the acquisition of the system function redundant. Most importantly, the simulation results have be validated on a real MPI scanner that is capable of performing both reconstruction techniques.

6 Conclusion

In this work the physical fundamentals of magnetic particle imaging have been presented. Magnetostatics, signal encoding, spatial encoding, the characteristics of the nanoparticles, the Lissajous trajectory, the prospect of resolution and sensitivity, and the signal chain of MPI have been discussed in detail. Further, the used simulation tool *scanner configuration* has been introduced along with three different scanner topologies the homogeneous, the classical, and the single-sided setup.

The frequency reconstruction has been explain theoretically while the measurement approach and the model-based approach were analysed with their advantages and drawbacks. It is explained how the system matrix is set up and discretized. Three of the most used techniques for solving a linear system of equation in MPI have been presented namely the least squares problem with Tikhonov regularization, the singular value decomposition, and the Karzmacz algorithm.

Afterwards, the x-space reconstruction technique has been studied in detail theoretically for the 1D case and the 3D case. Further, the x-space reconstruction has been illustrated in practise with a simple phantom and trajectory to clarify how the signal information is allocated to the pixel. The necessary deconvolution process for the x-space reconstruction has been explained with two different deconvolution techniques namely the deconvolution with Tikhonov regularization and the Wiener deconvolution.

As objective measurement, the normalized root mean square deviation is introduced to compare the results of each reconstruction method and further the theoretical advantages and disadvantages have been taken into consideration.

The results of comparing the two different deconvolution algorithms has clearly shown that the Wiener deconvolution yielded superior results in terms of visual inspection and magnitude of the NRMSD.

The comparison between the frequency and the x-space reconstruction has clearly shown that the frequency reconstruction provided better results with a less dense Lissajous trajectory and a lower sampling rate while keeping the 3D real-time condition. The x-space reconstruction showed promising results for a high dense Lissajous trajectory and a average sampling rate, but violated the real-time condition for 3D. In x-space further research will have to face the challenges of a high gradient with a homogeneous magnetic field for a large FOV and the hardware realization for the 3D real-time condition. Especially, the homogeneous magnetic will become challenging for the single-sided MPI scanner. If these challenges are solved, the x-space reconstruction can perform convincingly by having no system function and reconstructing the image on the fly.

In conclusion, the x-space reconstruction could provide an easy implementable and feasible reconstruction technique with the Lissajous trajectory when the scanner is modified to the prerequisites of x-space, but the accuracy of the frequency reconstruction will probably not be achieved.

The frequency reconstruction is more exact and has real-time ability, but remains impractical with its system function so far.

In the end, the practicability will lead the way for either or both techniques.

Bibliography

[1] B. Gleich and J. Weizenecker. Tomographic imaging using the nonlinear response of magnetic particles. *Nature*, 435(7046):1214–1217, Jun 2005.

[2] J. Weizenecker, J. Borgert, and B. Gleich. A simulation study on the resolution and sensitivity of magnetic particle imaging. *Phys Med Biol*, 52(21):6363–6374, Nov 2007.

[3] J. Weizenecker, B. Gleich, J. Rahmer, H. Dahnke, and J. Borgert. Three-dimensional real-time in vivo magnetic particle imaging. *Phys Med Biol*, 54(5):L1–L10, Mar 2009.

[4] R. W. Katzberg and C. Haller. Approaches to contrast-induced nephropathy. *Kidney Int.*, Suppl. S3, 2006.

[5] E. A. Neuwelt, B. E. Hamilton, C. G. Varallyay, W. R. Rooney, R. P. M. Jacobs, and S. G. Watnick. Ultrasmall superparamagnetic iron oxides (uspios): a future alternative magnetic resonance (mr) contrast agent for patients at risk for nephrogenic systemic fibrosis (nsf)? *Kidney Int.*, 75:465, 2009.

[6] M. Lu, M. H. Cohen, D. Rieves, and R. Pazdur. Fda report: Ferumoxytol for intravenous iron therapy in adult patients with chronic kidney disease. *Am. J. Hematol*, 85:315, 2010.

[7] D. Finas et al. Sentinal lymphnode detection in breast cancer by magnetic particle imaging using superparamagnetic nanoparticles. *International Workshop on Magnetic Particle Imaging BoA*, vol. 1:35, 2010.

[8] J. Haegele et al. Magnetic particle imaging: Visualization of instruments for cardiovascular intervention. *to be published in Radiology*.

[9] B. Gleich, J. Weizenecker, and J. Borgert. Experimental results on fast 2d-encoded magnetic particle imaging. *Phys Med Biol*, 53(6):N81–N84, Mar 2008.

[10] T. Sattel, T. Knopp, S. Biederer, B. Gleich, J. Weizenecker, J. Borgert, and T. M. Buzug. Single-sided device for magnetic particle imaging. *Journal of Physics D: Applied Physics*, 42(2):1–5, 2009.

[11] T. Knopp. *Effiziente Reconstruktion und alternative Topologien für Magnetic-Particle-Imaging*. Vieweg & Teuber, 2010.

[12] T. Knopp, T. F. Sattel, S. Biederer, J. Rahmer, J. Weizenecker, B. Gleich, J. Borgert, and T. M. Buzug. Model-based reconstruction for magnetic particle imaging. *IEEE Trans Med Imaging*, 29(1):12–18, Jan 2010.

[13] H. Schomberg. Magnetic particle imaging: Model and reconstruction. *in Proc. IEEE ISBI*, pages 992–995, 2010.

[14] P. W. Goodwill and S. M. Conolly. The x-space formulation of the magnetic particle imaging process: 1-d signal, resolution, bandwidth, snr, sar, and magnetostimulation. *IEEE Trans Med Imaging*, 29(11):1851–1859, Nov 2010.

[15] P. W. Goodwill, K. Lu, B. Zheng, and S. M. Conolly. An x-space magnetic particle imaging scanner. *Rev Sci Instrum*, 83(3):033708, Mar 2012.

[16] P. W. Goodwill, E. U. Saritas, L. R. Croft, T. N. Kim, K. M. Krishnan, D. V. Schaffer, and S. M. Conolly. X-space mpi: magnetic nanoparticles for safe medical imaging. *Adv Mater*, 24(28):3870–3877, Jul 2012.

[17] T. Knopp, S. Biederer, T. F. Sattel, J. Rahmer, J. Weizenecker, Bernhard Gleich, J. Borgert, and T. M. Buzug. 2d model-based reconstruction for magnetic particle imaging. *Med Phys*, 37(2):485–491, Feb 2010.

[18] G. Lehner. *Elektromagnetische Feldtheorie*. Berlin Springer, 2010.

[19] E. Rebhan. *Theoretische Physik: Elektrodynamik*. Elsevier Spectrum Akademischer Verlag, 2008.

[20] S. Biederer. *Magnet-Partikel-Spektrometer*. Vieweg & Teuber, 2012.

[21] T. Knopp, S. Biederer, T. Sattel, J. Weizenecker, B. Gleich, J. Borgert, and T. M. Buzug. Trajectory analysis for magnetic particle imaging. *Phys Med Biol*, 54(2):385–397, Jan 2009.

[22] L. Croft, P. Goodwill, and S. Conolly. Relaxation in x-space magnetic particle imaging. *IEEE Trans Med Imaging*, Sep 2012.

[23] P. W. Goodwill and S. M. Conolly. The x-space formulation of the magnetic particle imaging process: 1-d signal, resolution, bandwidth, snr, sar, and magnetostimulation. *IEEE Trans Med Imaging*, 29(11):1851–1859, Nov 2010.

[24] J. Rahmer, J. Weizenecker, B. Gleich, and J. Borgert. Signal encoding in magnetic particle imaging: properties of the system function. *BMC Med Imaging*, 9:4, 2009.

[25] J. Modersitzki. *FAIR: flexible algorithms for image registration*. SIAM, 2009.

[26] P. W. Goodwill and S. M. Conolly. Multidimensional x-space magnetic particle imaging. *IEEE Trans Med Imaging*, 30(9):1581–1590, Sep 2011.

[27] M. Grüttner. Image reconstruction in magnetic particle imaging. Oersund meets Hansebelt, 2012.

[28] J. Hadamard. Sur les problèmes aux dérivés partielles et leur signification physique. *Princeton University Bulletin*, 13:49–52, 1902.

[29] A. Tikhonov. Regularization of incorrectly posed problems. *Soviet Math. Dokl.*, 4:1624–1627, 1963.

[30] A. Tikhonov. Solution of incorrectly formulated problems and the regularization method. *Soviet Math. Dokl.*, 4:1036–1038, 1963.

[31] H. W. Engl and W. Grever. Using l-curve for determining optimal regularization parameters. *Numer. Math.*, 69:25–31, 1994.

[32] L. N. Trefethen and D. Bau. *Numerical linear algebra*. Philadelphia: Society for Industrial and Applied Mathematics, 1997.

[33] S. Kaczmarz. Angenäherte Auflösung von Aystemen linearer Gleichungen. *Bull. Internat. Acad. Polon. Sci. Let.*, A35:355–357, 1937.

[34] T. M. Buzug. *Computed Tomography: From Photon Statistics to Modern Cone Beam CT.* Springer Berlin Heidelberg, 2008.

[35] J. T. Marti. On the convergence of the discrete art algorithm for the reconstruction of digital pictures from their projections. *Computing*, 21(2):105–111, 1979.

[36] M. R. Trummer. Reconstructing pictures from projections: On the convergence of the art algorithm with relaxation. *Computing*, 26(3):189–195, 1981.

[37] L. Elsner, I. Koltracht, and P. Lancaster. Convergence properties of art and sor algorithms. *Numer. Math.*, 59(1):91–106, 1991.

[38] W. Norbert. Extrapolation, interpolation, and smoothing of stationary time series. *New York: Wiley*, 1949.

[39] J. S. Armstrong and F. Collopy. Error measures for generalizing about forecasting methods: Empirical comparisons. *International Journal of Forecasting*, 8:69–80, 1992.

[40] P. W. Goodwill, J. J. Konkle, B. Zheng, E. U. Saritas, and S. M. Conolly. Projection x-space magnetic particle imaging. *IEEE Trans Med Imaging*, 31(5):1076–1085, May 2012.

[41] 12.11.2012 dpa.   http://www.sueddeutsche.de/wissen/herz-und-psyche-blutsfeindschaft-
1.988810.

[42] T. M. Buzug, J. Weese, and C. Lorenz. Weighted least squares for point-based registration
in digital subtraction angiography (dsa). *Proc. SPIE*, 3661:139–150, 1999.

[43] M. Grüttner et al. 1d-image reconstruction for magnetic particle imaging using a hybrid
system function. *in Proc. IEEE Nuc. Sci. Symp. Med. Im. Conf.*, pages 2545–2548, 2011.

[44] A. Halkola, T. M. Buzug, J. Rahmer, B. Gleich, and C. Bontus. System calibration unit for
magnetic particle imaging: Focus field based system function. *in Springer Proceedings in
Physics Volume 140*, 42:27–31, 2012.

Infinite Science Publishing provides a publication platform for excellent theses as well as scientific monographies and conference proceedings for reasonable costs.

These publications enable scientists and research organizations to reach the maximum attention for their results.

The service of Infinite Science Publishing comprises the entire range from the publication of print-ready documents up to cover design as well as copy-editing of single articles.

Infinite Science Publishing is an imprint of the Infinite Science GmbH, a University of Lübeck spin-off and service partner of the BioMedTec Science Campus.

www.infinite-science.de/publishing

Infinite Science GmbH
MFC 1 | BioMedTec Wissenschaftscampus
Maria-Goeppert-Str. 1, 23562 Lübeck
book@infinite-science.de

Infinite Science
Publishing

More Titles on Magnetic Particle Imaging

Herstellung und
Charakterisierung
superparamagneti-
scher Lacke
*Inga Christine
Kuschnerus*
EUR 29,90

Optimierung der
Permanentmagne-
tengeometrie zur
Generierung eines
Selektionsfeldes für
Magnetic Particle
Imaging
Matthias Weber
EUR 29,90

Compressed Sen-
sing und Sparse
Rekonstruktion bei
Magnetic Particle
Imaging
Anselm von Gladiß
EUR 49,90

Beschleunigtes Mag-
netic Particle Ima-
ging: Untersuchung
des Einsatzes von
Compressed Sensing
für die Signalauf-
nahme
Nadine Traulsen
EUR 49,90

Power-Loss Opti-
mized Field-Free
Line Generation for
Magnetic Particle
Imaging
Matthias Weber
EUR 49,90

Elliptical Coils in
Magnetic Particle
Imaging
Christian Kaethner
EUR 49,90

 **Infinite Science Publishing**

www.infinite-science.de/publishing

Infinite Science GmbH
MFC 1 | BioMedTec Wissenschaftscampus
Maria-Goeppert-Str. 1, 23562 Lübeck
book@infinite-science.de